New Concepts for New Challenges

Professional Development for Teachers of Immigrant Youth

Printed in the United States of America
10 9 8 7 6 5 4 3 2 1

Topics in Immigrant Education 2

Editorial/production supervision: Joy Kreeft Peyton and Sonia Kundert
Copyediting: Sonia Kundert
Editorial/production assistance: Amy Fitch, Adriana Vaznaugh, and
    Lynn Fischer
Indexing: Kathleen McLane
Design and cover: SAGARTdesign
Cover photo: Dexter Dong Photography

ISBN 1-887744-04-5

The writing and production of the volumes in this series were supported in part by a grant from the Andrew W. Mellon Foundation, as one aspect of the Program in Immigrant Education. The opinions expressed in this report do not necessarily reflect the positions or policies of the Andrew W. Mellon Foundation.

Library of Congress Cataloging-in-Publication Data
González, Josué M., 1941-
     New concepts for new challenges : professional development for teachers of immigrant youth / Josué M. González and Linda Darling-Hammond.
          p.   cm. -- (Topics in immigrant education ; 2)
     Includes bibliographical references (p.   ) and index.
     ISBN 1-887744-04-5 (pbk.)
     1. Immigrants--Education (Secondary)--United States.
2. Children of immigrants--Education (Secondary)--United States.
3. Teachers--In-service training--United States.
     I. Darling-Hammond, Linda, 1951-   II. Title. III. Series.
     LC3731.G65   1997
     371.826'91--dc21
                                                            97-27403
                                                            CIP

New Concepts for New Challenges

Professional Development for Teachers of Immigrant Youth

Josué M. González & Linda Darling-Hammond
Teachers College, Columbia University

Topics in Immigrant Education Series

Series Editors:
Joy Kreeft Peyton and Donna Christian
Center for Applied Linguistics
Washington DC

Into, Through, and Beyond Secondary School:
Critical Transitions for Immigrant Youths
by Tamara Lucas

ISBN 1-887744-03-7

New Concepts for New Challenges:
Professional Development for Teachers of Immigrant Youth
by Josué M. González & Linda Darling-Hammond

ISBN 1-776644-04-5

Through the Golden Door:
Educational Approaches for Immigrant Adolescents With Limited
Schooling
by Betty J. Mace-Matluck, Rosalind Alexander-Kasparik,
& Robin M. Queen

ISBN 1-887744-07-X

Access and Engagement:
Program Design and Instructional Approaches for Immigrant
Students in Secondary School
by Aída Walqui

ISBN 1-887744-09-6

After a hiatus of half a century, a wave of immigration is once again transforming the United States. With over a million immigrants, legal and illegal, entering the United States each year, the foreign born constitute the fastest-growing segment of our population, reaching 24.5 million in 1996, roughly 10% of the population, the highest proportion since World War II (U.S. Bureau of the Census, 1997).

Even more striking than the scale of immigration is its makeup. Since the passage of the Immigration Act of 1965, which eliminated national origin quotas, Asia and Latin America have replaced Europe as the main sources of newcomers to the United States. The largest groups come from Mexico (accounting for 27.2% of the 1996 foreign-born population), China, Cuba, India, and Vietnam.

New immigrants to the United States come with diverse languages, cultures, and experiences, even within these larger groups. Asian immigrants, for example, include people from more than 13 countries in South, Southeast, and East Asia as well as the Pacific Islands. A single nationality can include several ethnic groups, each with a distinctive language and culture. A Laotian immigrant might be an ethnic Lao or a member of the Hmong, Mien, or Khmu ethnic minorities. An Asian Indian immigrant might be a Punjabi-speaking Sikh, a Bengali-speaking Hindu, or an Urdu-speaking Moslem.

While the great majority of Latin American immigrants share a common language, and to some extent a common culture, this group also displays a great diversity that is due to the various ancestries—European, African, and Native American—and nations represented. Recent Latin American immigrants have arrived chiefly from Mexico, El Salvador, Guatemala, Nicaragua, and Honduras. Caribbeans, arriving in smaller numbers, come mostly from Haiti, the Dominican Republic, Jamaica, and Cuba.

Today's immigrants also vary in their social and educational backgrounds and personal experiences. They come from the elite as well as the most disadvantaged sectors of their societies. Some left to escape poverty; others were fleeing war or political persecution; others were attracted by the hope for better educational and economic opportunities. Some came directly to the United States; others arrived after harrowing escapes followed by years in refugee camps.

Immigrant Students in America's Schools

While immigration has affected all aspects of American life, nowhere is the changing demography of the United States more keenly felt than in education. First- and second-generation immigrant children are the fastest-growing segment of the U.S. population under age 15 (Fix & Zimmerman, 1993). The 1990 U.S. Census counted 2.1 million foreign-born children in the United States. If children born in the United States to immigrant parents are included, the total is 5 million. By 2010, if current trends continue, 9 million school-age children will be immigrants or children of immigrants, representing 22% of the school-age population (Fix & Passel, 1994).

With over 90% of recent immigrants coming from non-English-speaking countries, schools are increasingly receiving students who do not speak English at home and who have little or no proficiency in English. There has been an increase of almost 1 million English learners in U.S. public schools (grades K-12) in the last 10 years, approximately 5.5% of the public school student population (Fleischman & Hopstock, 1993). It is difficult to determine the number who are considered limited English proficient (LEP, the term used by the federal government and most states) because states determine numbers of LEP students in different ways (Gándara, 1994). However, according to the 1993-94 Schools and Staffing Survey (National Center for Education Statistics, 1997), over 2.1 million public school students in the United States are identified as LEP. They account for 5% of all public school students and 31% of all American Indian/Alaska Native, Asian/Pacific Islander, and Hispanic students enrolled in public schools. The largest proportion of this population (over 79%) are native Spanish speakers (see Goldenberg, 1996). California has been particularly affected. The number of students classified as LEP in the state's public schools more than tripled from nearly 400,000 in 1981 to nearly 1.3 million in 1995 (California Department of Education, 1995). These students were reported to speak one or more of 54 different primary languages.

Along with an increase in sheer numbers of immigrant students who are at various stages of learning English, schools are also faced with an increasing number of students needing extra academic instruction in addition to English as a second language (ESL) classes. Approximately 20% of all English language learners at the high school level and 12% at the middle school level have missed two or more years of schooling since the age of six; 27% in high school and 19% in middle school are assigned to grades at least two years lower than age/grade norms (Fleischman & Hopstock, 1993).

Because newcomers to this country tend to concentrate in certain areas, the responsibility for educating immigrant students is not evenly shared across the country. According to the 1993-94 Schools and Staffing Survey, 82% of the LEP students in K-12 public schools live in only five states—California, Texas, New York, Florida, and Illinois; more than 40% are in California. Dade County, Florida, is an example of a school system struggling to serve a sudden, relatively recent influx of immigrants. Approximately a quarter of the 330,000 students in Dade County, Florida, in Fall 1996 were born outside the United States (Schnaiberg, 1996), and the county adds an average of 1,322 foreign-born students a month to its rolls. At the same time, employment opportunities draw immigrants to smaller cities and even rural areas as well, creating new challenges for schools in those areas.

An increasingly diverse student population is hitting the schools at the same time as a record number of students in general (the *baby boom echo*, a term used by demographers referring to children of the original baby boomers) are entering school. In the fall of 1996, over 51 million children entered school, a new national record (U.S. Department of Education, 1996). The Department of Education predicts that numbers of students enrolled in school will not level off until 2006, when they reach 54.6 million, almost 3 million more than in 1996. The

greatest increase over the next decade will be in high school enrollments, projected to increase by 15%. Thus, schools already struggling
with the influx of immigrant students are also facing the strains of high
overall enrollments.

Understanding the Immigrant Student Population

In this series, the term *immigrant* includes those students (including
refugees) born outside the United States, but not those born and raised
in non-English speaking homes within the United States. Within this
group, the focus is on English language learners who are in ESL or bilingual classes, those who no longer have access to ESL or bilingual
services but are having trouble in academic classes taught in English,
and those who are literate in their native language as well as those who
are not. Because the series focuses on students for whom secondary
school is a reasonable placement, students' ages range from 9 to 21
years.

U.S.-born secondary school students enter school at age 5 or 6 and, if
they remain in school, follow a fairly predictable sequence of
coursework. Educators can, therefore, assume certain experiences and
knowledge among those students. However, no such assumptions can
be made about adolescent immigrant students' educational backgrounds and readiness for secondary schooling in the United States.
Immigrant students arrive at all ages. They may have had an educational preparation superior to that provided by most U.S. schools, or
they may have had no previous educational experience at all. Thus,
different educational approaches are called for with these students—
for example, a 15-year-old who immigrated from Mexico at age 13
with a strong educational background, one who immigrated at age 13
with only two years of prior schooling, and one who immigrated at age
7 and entered school immediately.

Many additional factors can affect immigrant students' adjustment to
U.S. schooling and their success in the transition from adolescence to
adulthood. These include individual and family characteristics, the

similarities and differences between their native countries and cultures and the United States, their immigration experiences, and the contexts in which they live in the United States. (See Tamara Lucas's volume in this series, pages 18, 19, 114, and 115.) Knowledge of these factors can form the foundation upon which educators build programs and approaches that will assist these students in making their way through school and on to postsecondary school or work.

Facing the Challenges

The demographic realities described above are cause for serious concern, and many educators believe that the education system in the United States is poorly prepared to meet the needs of its linguistically and culturally diverse student population. Gándara (1994) claims that English language learners were sidelined in the first wave of reform efforts during the 1980s, and a report by the Stanford Working Group (1993) calls the nation's school systems to task for failing to provide these students with equitable educational opportunities. Moss and Puma (1995) found that English language learners receive lower grades and are judged by their teachers to have lower academic abilities than native-born students, and they score below their native-English-speaking classmates on standardized tests of reading and math.

The challenges of educating immigrant students and English language learners are especially acute at the secondary school level. As Chips (1993) argues, immigrant students of secondary school age can face major difficulties in acquiring English and succeeding in school. If they are newcomers to the United States, they have much less time than elementary age students to learn English and master the academic content required to graduate from high school. They must pass tests that require English skills that they do not have. They must study subjects such as physical science, chemistry, economics, and geometry that require high levels of English academic language. Most secondary school texts and materials require a high level of English reading ability. Few schools provide native-language support for these classes, English-language instruction tied to content, or content classes taught with adaptations of English appropriate for these students' levels of proficiency. Students learning English often find it difficult to be accepted in well-established groups of English-speaking students. Finally, students who hope to attend college or university after high school face even greater challenges, as they attempt to succeed in classes designated for college credit and to master the maze of requirements for college acceptance.

High dropout rates among language-minority secondary school students are just one indication that many schools are failing to meet the challenge. For example, Hispanic students are more likely than White students to leave school during their high school years (10% versus 4%; National Center for Education Statistics, 1996). In 1994, the number of Hispanic students aged 16–24 who had not completed high school and were not enrolled was 30%, as compared to 8% for White students (Lockwood, 1996). Certain subgroups of Asian refugee populations also have high dropout rates; a study of dropout rates in California schools found that those schools with high concentrations of Southeast Asians had the highest dropout rates (U.S. Commission on Civil Rights, 1992).

A number of factors underlie the failure of secondary schools to serve the needs of immigrant students. These include

- a school structure that does not facilitate smooth transitions from program to program, school to school, or school to college or work;
- an instructional program that fails to give them access to academic concepts and skills;
- few program and curricular alternatives for students with limited prior schooling and low literacy skills; and
- a shortage of school personnel trained to meet their specific needs.

These factors characterize an educational system that has failed to keep up with its changing population, particularly at the secondary school level. At the same time, relatively little research is available on effective approaches to educating students at this level (August & Hakuta, 1997).

Books in This Series

The books in this series address these issues, providing profiles of immigrant students from a variety of backgrounds, critical reviews of what we know from the research that is available, and descriptions of programs that show promise.

New Concepts for New Challenges: Professional Development for Teachers of Immigrant Youth, **by Josué M. González and Linda Darling-Hammond (with Elsie Szecsy, Kavemuii Murangi, & David Jacobson)**

Because of immigrant students' diverse backgrounds and needs, school staff need specialized preparation to work effectively with them. It is increasingly clear that all teachers with immigrant students and English language learners in their classes need to know about second language development, cross-cultural issues, and methods to teach both language and academic content. However, most classroom teachers, counselors, and administrators receive no special training in these areas. Although the number of university programs offering specialization in ESL and bilingual education has increased during the past decade, there remains a shortage of qualified ESL and bilingual education specialists. The National Center for Education Statistics (1997) reported that only 2.5% of teachers in the United States who instruct English language learners have an academic degree in ESL or bilingual education; only 30% of the teachers with these students in their classes have received any training at all in teaching them.

In addition, school staff have limited opportunities to update their knowledge and skills on an ongoing basis. The traditional model for inservice professional development—brief workshops on various topics and strategies, presented by "experts" from outside the school—cannot provide school personnel with more than a superficial understanding of the needs of immigrant students. Substantial changes in teaching practice are likely to occur only when teachers receive extended opportunities throughout the year to reflect on their practice and work with colleagues to improve it. These opportunities must be considered a natural and necessary part of professional growth rather than a remedial activity.

In this book, the second in this series, González and Darling-Hammond describe the challenges to developing a teaching force that is competent to work with immigrant students. They argue that we need to rethink professional development and move far beyond traditional "inservicing" and "teacher training." They develop a framework for considering what teachers of immigrant youth need to understand about their students, what kinds of professional development experiences are likely to facilitate those understandings, and what kinds of teacher education programs and school settings are able to support their ongoing learning. They argue that professional development needs to occur in preservice education; during induction, when new teachers are adjusting to being part of the staff of a school; and throughout teachers' careers. They describe promising new structures and practices for professional development, focusing particularly on those that promote community, collegiality, and collaboration. Finally, they profile innovative approaches to preservice and inservice professional development in California, Maryland, Minnesota, and New York.

Into, Through, and Beyond Secondary School: Critical Transitions for Immigrant Youths, **by Tamara Lucas**

Immigrant adolescents who enter U.S. schools with limited proficiency in English must negotiate a series of critical transitions in order to progress through school. At the same time that they are dealing with the difficult developmental transitions from childhood to adolescence to adulthood, they also must make the transitions from their native country to the United States; from middle school to high school; from bilingual and ESL classes to content area classes; and from high school to postsecondary education or work. In this book, Lucas argues that in order for schools to help immigrant students make these transitions successfully, we must apply the best knowledge we have about teaching, learning, and schooling. We must reconceptualize our notions of learners and learning, teachers and teaching, and schools and schooling. Lucas discusses four specific principles that secondary school staff can apply to facilitate these reconceptualizations and to promote students' transitions—cultivate organizational relationships; provide access to information; cultivate human relationships; and provide multiple and flexible pathways into, through, and beyond secondary school. She provides a set of questions that school staff can use to guide them in establishing effective practices within each principle, and she describes programs in which these principles have been implemented.

Through the Golden Door: Educational Approaches for Immigrant Adolescents With Limited Schooling, by Betty Mace-Matluck, Rosalind Alexander-Kasparik, and Robin M. Queen

A growing number of recent immigrant students enter middle and high school with little or no prior formal schooling. Often referred to as "late-entrant" or "low-literacy," these students are between the ages of 9 and 21 and are three years or more below their age-appropriate grade level. As a result, they often do not have time to fulfill high school graduation requirements before they reach the state's maximum age for high school attendance. In this book, the authors profile five such students (from Haiti, El Salvador, and Vietnam), describe in detail four programs designed to serve them (in Illinois, Texas, and Virginia), identify critical features of secondary school programs for them, and give program contact information and resources.

Access and Engagement: Program Design and Instructional Approaches for Immigrant Students in Secondary School, by Aída Walqui

In this book, Aída Walqui describes features of secondary schools in the United States that make it difficult for immigrant students to succeed. These include fragmented school days, fragmented instructional programs in which ESL and content area teachers work in separate departments and rarely interact, the complex system of courses and of graduation and college entrance requirements, the practice of placing students in grades according to their age, and the use of traditional methods of documenting student achievement. She profiles six immigrant high school students (from Brazil, El Salvador, Haiti, Mexico, Russia, and Vietnam) and the challenges they face in school; describes the philosophies, designs, and instructional approaches of four programs (in California, Iowa, and New York) attempting to address these challenges; and proposes 10 characteristics of schools and programs that can foster effective teaching and learning for immigrant youth.

Conclusion

New visions of learning, teaching, and schooling push us to break through the traditional boundaries of the classroom and the school to redefine who participates in teaching and learning, in what ways they participate, and where resources for teaching and learning reside. Immigrant students must be included in the population of *all* students whom school reform movements and new approaches to schooling are designed to serve. We can no longer develop programs that ignore the needs of these students and deprive them of the benefits of broad educational reforms. The education of immigrant students needs to sit squarely within the educational reform movement, so that those students of secondary school age have access to high-quality programs in school and postsecondary opportunities beyond school, and the opportunity to become productive members of our society.

To do this, we need strong, responsive school programs and practices that provide opportunities for immigrant students to learn academic content while they are learning English, that smooth their transitions through and beyond school, and that are sensitive to the special needs of students with limited prior schooling and low literacy skills. Educators of these students need to understand the principles and practices of educational reform and participate in the design and implementation of new programs and approaches. Finally, all educators must develop culturally and linguistically responsive understandings and skills to facilitate the success of all of their students.

Series Acknowledgments

The Program in Immigrant Education, begun in 1993, was funded by The Andrew W. Mellon Foundation to improve immigrant students' access to high-quality education in secondary school, their success in school, and their transitions to education and work after high school. Demonstration projects in Northern California, Southern California, Maryland, and Texas were established to implement, document, and evaluate innovative projects to accomplish these general goals.

This book series was developed to inform project staff as well as researchers and practitioners working with immigrant students about topics that are critical to this effort. After extensive conversations with project directors and staff, advisors to the program, and leaders in the field of immigrant education, priority topics were identified. For each topic, authors were asked to review what is known, document promising programs, and identify available resources.

We are grateful for the input we received on topics, authors, and book content from project staff Albert Cortez, JoAnn Crandall, Ann Jaramillo, Laurie Olsen, and David Ramírez; program advisors Keith Buchanan, Margarita Calderón, Eugene García, Victoria Jew, Eric Nadelstern, and Delia Pompa; and colleagues Michelle Brewer Byrd, Russell Campbell, Rosa Castro Feinberg, Kenji Hakuta, Tamara Lucas, Betty Mace-Matluck, Denise McKeon, and G. Richard Tucker. We extend special thanks to Tamara Lucas, who provided information included in the introduction; to Sonia Kundert, who coordinated the books' production; to Lynn Fischer and Amy Fitch, who provided editorial assistance; and to Adriana Vaznaugh for collecting information and communicating with authors. Finally, we are grateful to Stephanie Bell-Rose, program officer at The Andrew W. Mellon Foundation, for her support of the work of the Program in Immigrant Education.

Joy Kreeft Peyton and Donna Christian, Series Editors

References

August, D., & Hakuta, K. (1997). *Improving schooling for language-minority children: A research agenda*. Washington, DC: National Academy Press.

California Department of Education, Educational Demographics Unit. (1995). *Language census report for California public schools 1995*. Sacramento, CA: Author.

Chips, B. (1993). Using cooperative learning at the secondary level. In D.D. Holt (Ed.), *Cooperative learning: A response to linguistic and cultural diversity* (pp. 81-97). McHenry, IL and Washington, DC: Delta Systems and Center for Applied Linguistics.

Fix, M., & Passel, J.S. (1994). *Immigration and immigrants: Setting the record straight*. Washington, DC: The Urban Institute.

Fix, M., & Zimmerman, W. (1993). *Educating immigrant children: Chapter 1 in the changing city*. Washington, DC: The Urban Institute.

Fleischman, H.L., & Hopstock, P.J. (1993). *Descriptive study of services to limited English proficient students. Vol. 1: Summary of findings and conclusions*. Arlington, VA: Development Associates.

Gándara, P. (1994). The impact of the education reform movement on limited English proficient students. In B. McLeod (Ed.), *Language and learning: Educating linguistically diverse students* (pp. 45-70). Albany, NY: SUNY Press.

Goldenberg, C. (1996). Latin American immigration and U.S. schools. *Social Policy Report, 10*(1), 1-29. Ann Arbor, MI: Society for Research in Child Development.

Lockwood, A.T. (1996, Summer). Caring, community, and personalization: Strategies to combat the Hispanic dropout problem. *Advances in Hispanic Education: U.S. Department of Education/Hispanic Drop-out Project, No. 1* [Online]. Available: http://www.ncbe.gwu.edu/miscpubs/used/advances/s96no1.html [1996, November 14].

Moss, M., & Puma, M. (1995). *Prospects: The Congressionally mandated study of educational growth and opportunity.* Cambridge, MA: Abt Associates.

National Center for Education Statistics. (1996). *Dropout rates in the United States: 1994* (NCES 96-863). Washington, DC: U.S. Government Printing Office.

National Center for Education Statistics. (1997). *A profile of policies and practices for limited English proficient students: Screening methods, program support, and teacher training [SASS 1993-94]* (NCES 97-472). Washington, DC: U.S. Government Printing Office.

Schnaiberg, L. (1996, September 11). Immigration plays key supporting role in record-enrollment drama. *Education Week, 16,* 24-25.

Stanford Working Group. (1993). *Federal education programs for limited-English-proficient students: A blueprint for the second generation.* Stanford, CA: Stanford University.

U.S. Bureau of the Census. (1997). *The foreign-born population: 1996* [Online]. Available: http://www.census.gov/population/www/socdemo/foreign96.html [1997, April 15].

U.S. Commission on Civil Rights. (1992, February). *Civil rights issues facing Asian Americans in the 1990s.* Washington, DC: Author.

U.S. Department of Education. (1996, August). *A back to school special report: The baby boom echo.* Washington, DC: Author.

In the preparation of this volume, we interviewed many people and observed practice in the sites that illustrate best practice. We appreciate the insights provided by Joy Peyton, Deborah Short, and Sonia Kundert at the Center for Applied Linguistics. Their suggestions and comments enriched this work. We also thank all of the other people who enriched our understanding of the field sites that are represented here.

We also relied heavily on the greater educational community for advisory assistance. The authors of the companion books in the series—Tamara Lucas, Betty Mace-Matluck, and Aída Walqui—offered many helpful insights, as did members of the Advisory Committee to the Program in Immigrant Education—Margarita Calderón and Eric Nadelstern—and members of the review panel for this volume—Charlene Rivera, Marietta Saravia-Shore, and Claire Sylvan. These individuals were especially helpful in reviewing and commenting on the first draft. We are most grateful for opportunities to listen to and learn from practitioners and other researchers. Their insights have been incorporated into and have enriched this volume.

Finally, we very greatly appreciate the efforts of the cadre of research assistants at Teachers College, Columbia University—Elsie Szecsy, Kavemuii Murangi, and David Jacobson—for their work in identifying and integrating the research literature that supports this volume and for drafting and reviewing the manuscript with us throughout its development. These three individuals did far more than graduate students are expected to do, and this book bears their imprint.

The demographics of the nation's immigrants are changing. Immigration from Asia and Latin America is increasing at a steady rate, while immigration from Europe has slowed considerably. According to 1990 U.S. Census statistics, though the general population increased in size by 9.8% in the decade ending in 1990, the Asian population grew by 107.8%, the Latino population by 53.0%. These trends show no sign of reversing themselves in the future. The immigrants represented in these statistics are not limited to historical immigrant ports of entry. Their presence is being felt in increasing numbers in many states (e.g., *The Road to College*, 1991).

The effects of the changing demographics of the United States are also being felt by a larger number of teachers than ever before. In the past, high concentrations of immigrant families tended to be found only in the major port cities, and their children were concentrated in the schools of those same urban centers. In traditional ports of entry, such as New York City, the proportion of immigrants is perhaps no larger than it was at the start of the 20th century. The city's immigrant population is, however, much more diverse (from a greater range of nations, regions, and cultures) than it has been in the past. In addition, today's immigrant populations are dispersed throughout the United States and represent a significant proportion of many more communities (Roberts, 1993). Teachers in suburban and rural communities, who previously were insulated from these students, find themselves in the difficult position of teaching groups of students with whom they have little experience and for whom they have little preparation. As the presence of immigrant students is felt in schools nationwide, there is more pressure on school staff to examine instructional practices and to reexamine assumptions regarding the purpose of education and the meanings that schools ascribe to cultural and linguistic pluralism, to the relationship between teacher and learner, and to the social environment that influences those relationships (González, 1993).

This volume examines how professional learning opportunities can be strengthened for teachers of immigrant adolescents. We develop a framework for exploring what teachers need to understand about their students, what kinds of professional learning experiences are likely to support those understandings, and what kinds of school settings and teacher education programs are able to support teacher learning. While we focus particularly on the education of adolescents, we frame our discussion around the education of all immigrant students. And while we focus on professional development for teachers, we also touch on issues of professional development for other members of the educational community.

Overview of the Volume

In this introduction, we have described briefly how the sociocultural and linguistic profile of the nation's student population is changing. We note the important phenomenon of national dispersal, the fact that these changes are no longer limited to immigrant ports of entry. Immigration influxes into schools and communities are now a nationwide phenomenon. Where previously there were few families from ethnic minorities, ethnic and national origin minorities now represent a significant proportion of the population. In a growing number of cities and small communities, large segments of minority group students have arrived only recently as immigrants.

These changes are having a profound effect on the schools attended by children and adolescents whose life experiences and language may differ markedly from those of classmates who are not immigrants. In chapter 1, we give a short history of cultural diversity in the United States and point out how educational conditions are different for today's immigrants. We focus attention on characteristics of immigrant students and the cultural and sociopolitical factors that may encourage or impede teachers' efforts to meet the needs of these students. We examine structural limitations of schools that inhibit the redesign of teaching and teacher learning opportunities. Finally, we discuss the features of schools that are working effectively with linguistically and culturally diverse students and the implications for professional development of teachers.

Immigrant students often bring different perspectives to the schools they attend than those of students who have attended U.S. schools in the past. Their perspectives are a mix of different ways of seeing themselves as students, subtle and not-so-subtle ways of perceiving the role of teachers, and different ways of becoming motivated to learn and achieve. These differences can provide a rich experience for all learners, immigrants or not. They can also cause frustration among teachers who are not ready to deal with this diversity. Often, the extent of diversity and range of perspectives are greater among immigrant students than among their teachers. Chapter 1 focuses on the sociocultural and linguistic characteristics of diversity and its implications for teaching, learning, and professional development. It briefly reviews research on what is known about teaching strategies that support the language development and academic success of immigrant students.

Chapter 2 focuses on the continuing education needs of teachers and the need to rethink professional development in ways that go beyond traditional "inservicing" or "teacher training." Professional development needs to occur in preservice education; during induction, when teachers are adjusting to being part of the staff of a school; and throughout teachers' careers. The demographics of the American teaching force do not resemble the demographics of the students whom teachers encounter in their classrooms. This creates a need for teachers to continually reexamine what school means in the context of cultural and linguistic pluralism, the relationship between teacher and learner, and the ways in which social pressures of the peer group influence that relationship. We examine professional growth opportunities that address teachers' attitudes and beliefs about the nature and purpose of schooling and their attitudes about relating to and understanding immigrant students.

Chapter 3 explores promising new structures, models, and practices for professional development. Older conceptions of staff development and the acquisition of skills for delivering instruction are being replaced by new ideas, which are very different from and more effective than older models. These new concepts call into question the efficacy of a system that relies solely on diagnostic-prescriptive aspects of typical skills-oriented staff development offerings. They suggest a need to redefine the roles of teachers, supervisors, and administrators in deciding what forms and types of training and development opportunities to offer and who should carry them out. They redefine the relationship of school personnel to universities and other providers of pre- and inservice education, the format of these experiences, and even the wisdom of using "experts" to conduct such activities. In this chapter, we present a synthesis of contemporary recommendations for facilitating inservice professional growth. Special attention is given to the manner in which new concepts of professional development suit the needs of teachers of immigrants.

We also look explicitly at the emergence of new mindsets and structures that promote community, collegiality, and collaboration among teachers, administrators, and others involved in the design of professional development options for educators who work with language minority students. We suggest that traditional notions of pedagogy may limit the development of immigrant adolescents' skills in English, because they limit interaction among students and teachers. For example, traditional forms of curriculum and teaching assume a predisposition among students to complete class work in ways that immigrant students may not be accustomed to or comfortable with. Teacher-centered instruction limits opportunities for students to use language in authentic contexts. Professional development opportunities (such as cooperative learning, problem-based inquiry, peer and cognitive coaching, team teaching, and home–school collaboration) that break the diagnostic-prescriptive training model for teachers and offer opportunities for teachers to learn in a more collaborative model will provide opportunities for richer communication among them. Having experienced collaborative learning themselves, it will be easier for teachers of immigrant students to implement the same model among their students. Professional development opportunities that focus on student characteristics provide important knowledge that will facilitate richer experiences for immigrant students in the classrooms of educators who may be unfamiliar with their cultural backgrounds.

Adding this type of professional development fills the existing lacuna in most current staff development program repertoires.

Chapter 4 profiles three preservice and two inservice programs that show promise for developing teachers' abilities to work effectively with immigrant youth. Preservice professional development programs described are The Second Languages and Cultures Education program at the University of Minnesota and the Cross-Cultural Language and Academic Development (CLAD) teacher preparation programs at San Diego State University and at the University of California, Santa Barbara. Exemplary inservice programs described are The International High School in New York City, and the Bilingual Cooperative Integrated Reading and Composition (BCIRC) Model used in a number of schools and districts around the United States.

In the concluding chapter, we pull together the threads that run through the volume—the social and cyclical nature of learning, the need for an anthropological orientation in understanding students and the teachers who work with them, and the promise of video and other technology to help school staff view and reflect on their work.

The Changing Context for Educating Immigrants

A Historical Perspective on Cultural Diversity in the United States

Attention to issues related to cultural diversity in the United States is not a new phenomenon. Zelasko (1991) cites a number of studies, each of which identified different frameworks reflecting the variety of attitudes toward immigration and language differences over the course of the nation's history from 1777. For example, use of languages other than English in education has ranged from being openly accepted to reluctantly tolerated at different points in history and in different parts of the nation. These shifting attitudes have, to a great extent, been driven by the economic realities of the times. For example, immigration has been encouraged during periods in our history to boost the American economy. While menial labor was unattractive to many mainstream Americans, for immigrants it was often the only pathway to assimilation into the American culture. There is a pervasive view of immigrants as a class of unskilled workers whose children find it as difficult to learn as their parents find it difficult to enter the economic mainstream. Stereotypes endure. Our expectations of immigrants are often far lower than they should be. In fact, there are more ways of "becoming American" today than there were in previous decades.

Language is an instructive example. Language and literacy can be seen as instruments of economic, cultural, and political power. Thus it was not uncommon in an earlier period of American history for the language of the most powerful group to be the preferred mode of communication for a particular settlement. For example, in the 1850s, beginning in Wisconsin, a number of states in the Midwest passed laws prohibiting the use of German or, in some cases, any foreign language in school or other public places (Hakuta, 1986; Kloss, 1977/in press). Public policy decisions regarding immigration and language were often motivated by economic and political concerns of those in power.

Approximately 75% of the persons polled in a recent Gallup Poll of the Public's Attitudes Toward the Public Schools (Elam, Rose, & Gallup,

1994) felt that the public schools in their communities should promote both one common tradition and the diverse traditions of different populations. More than half felt that there should be equal emphasis on both. At the same time, public policy actions such as the passing of Proposition 187 in California in November 1994 suggest an attitude toward immigrants that borders on hostility in some places (Immigrant Policy Project, 1995; see also Brimelow, 1995). Therefore, while the sentiments of some sectors of society appear to place pressure on schools to provide exposure to diverse traditions, attempts of other sectors to influence public policy may send a contradictory message. This difference signals our continuing national ambivalence toward ethnic, cultural, and linguistic diversity (Steinberg, 1989) and the pedagogical meanings attached to these concepts.

Americans have not always been hostile to languages other than English. As Hakuta (1986) and Kloss (1977/in press) point out, throughout much of the history of the United States, the preservation of one's ethnic language has been regarded as a social skill as well as a legitimate attempt to preserve one's ethnic identity. In the early colonies, instruction in several languages was commonplace and supported primarily by religious institutions as a means to preserve family and religious traditions. Native language instruction rarely became a public policy issue. This history explains, in part, the sometimes conflicting values placed on multilingualism in this country today. The rich linguistic diversity that has always been a part of this country's tradition has been valued, but only in certain aspects of private life and rarely as a means of public discourse. The assumption has always been that English was to predominate as the language of discourse, and all other languages were subordinate to it. This principle has been played out repeatedly throughout our history.

Though our history is replete with instances of ethnic diversity and multilingualism, what separates the historical context from the present situation is that most of the earlier non-English-speaking immigrants were White and European. They immigrated intentionally to escape oppression or economic hardship and viewed exchanging their language for the English language as a necessary part of becoming American. For the most part, they were separated from their home culture by the broad expanses of physical distance and slow communications and travel. There are indications too that White immigrants were more favorably disposed to intermarry with other White groups, thereby contributing to a White-dominant or Eurocentric culture.

Recent waves of immigrants have tended to have a different orientation to their respective languages. Many new immigrants are Asian, Latin American, and Caribbean. They are people of color, whose cultures are rooted in Amerindian, Buddhist, and Confucian ways of thinking and who want to integrate their home cultures with the culture of their new home. Perhaps this feeling exists because modern means of travel and communication make the maintenance of ancestral languages and cultures more immediately possible. Unlike previous generations of immigrants, the current wave can maintain contact with the home culture and grow with it from a distance in ways that were not possible before the availability of the Internet and satellite television technologies. Immediate access to the home culture from remote stations facilitates ongoing contact and motivates immigrants to maintain their cultural identities. This is a different pattern from that of previous waves of immigrants, who appeared to preserve in their memories the culture they brought with them, but who were not able to maintain contact with their home culture.

Because they are the premier instrument of acculturation, American schools will continue to play an important role in helping to knit diverse groups into the national culture. It seems fairly apparent, however, that in the 21st century, schools cannot expect to carry out that function in a unidirectional, assimilationist mode. School staff must learn to respect and celebrate cultural differences and to understand those cultural and linguistic elements that immigrants may wish to retain, at the same time that immigrant students learn to function effectively in a new social and cultural environment. Arguably, language is the most visible aspect of student diversity that schools encounter and that school staff are least prepared to address in a manner that demonstrates reciprocal respect.

It can be argued that schools must become as diverse as the students they serve. Leaders of American education spent the 20th century designing a unitary and homogeneous system of schools. Leaders of the 21st century may need to do the opposite: create schools that embrace diversity and are themselves diverse in order to meet the challenges of diverse populations. It seems fairly clear that Americans, including educators, can no longer assume that the price of citizenship and social acceptance is the abandonment of old ways in favor of a replacement culture. In some cases, immigrants bring old rivalries and religious divisions that play themselves out in the new homeland. For some of these old enemies, the United States is not just a place to make a fresh new start; it is also a new theater for their old wars. It can also be a place where such conflicts will end, but that may take time. Because the schools are the place where the children of these groups will meet and interact, teachers must be more skilled than ever, not only in techniques of teaching but also in human relations, creative problem solving, and conflict resolution. These skills will be far more important in the schools of the future than they have ever been in the past.

Immigrants as Individuals

When developing ways to improve the education of immigrant students, it is helpful to bear in mind the immigrant student as an individual. Teachers and administrators must develop an understanding of and sensitivity to the individual immigrant as a member of the general school community as well as a member of his or her ethnic or language group. We urge caution in making generalizations about the needs of immigrant students and therefore about the solutions to educational concerns. Understanding is the product of knowledge, skills, and dispositions which, in the aggregate, lead to a greater sensitivity concerning immigrant students. Traditional conceptions of professional preparation have sometimes emphasized static skills and knowledge at the expense of the third factor—a predisposition to attend to the needs of the learner, which leads to a willingness to do things differently when the needs of the learner require it.

Immigrant children and youth do not share common experiences or identical histories, although we sometimes use the phrase "immigrant experience" as if they did. Many people assume that all immigrants pay the same price of admission into American society. In fact, immigrant children are diverse among themselves. They include those who have been traumatized by the ravages of war, famine, and persecution as well as those who come from the privileged oligarchies of the world. Immigrants come to U.S. schools with varying degrees of prior schooling or no schooling at all. While some have suffered more than others prior to coming here, all experience some level of trauma and change in adjusting to another culture, a different language, and a world view that may be distinct from their own. The collective effect of these life changes may cause frustration and anxiety. Their experiences can have cultural, academic, and psychological implications for both the immigrant and the school, although we cannot assume that deep personal trauma is a characteristic shared by all immigrant students. In short, teachers must be prepared to meet many manifestations of the immigrant experience and adapt their teaching and support functions to the numerous ways of being an immigrant.

It is equally important to understand the various stages of uprooting and adaptation that immigrant students experience. When they first learn of the impending relocation to another country, soon-to-be immigrant children may have mixed emotions. They may get excited or fearful about the adventure that looms ahead and curious about what life will be like in their new home. Once arrived, many experience the frustration of not understanding or being understood. Their reactions to language and cultural differences may range from mild puzzlement to deep depression. Wherever they may be on this continuum, it is likely that classmates and peers will be an important part of their adaptation. Sensitive teachers make provision for the helping hands of peers to be extended.

In subsequent stages of adaptation, the immigrant student considers the difficulties of assimilation and acculturation. Assimilation requires trading the old for the new; acculturation permits the retention of the old culture and the addition of the new. Teachers who encourage the latter are encouraging the development of a whole individual who can move into the mainstream with the knowledge of both where he or she comes from and where he or she is going. When teachers understand the process of integration into the national culture, they can interpret student behaviors more accurately. One example of this is the silence that many immigrant children and youth display when they first enter American schools. Knowledge of the difficulties that these students are experiencing as they encounter a different language and culture can empower teachers to act with greater confidence in helping them adjust.

In her conversations with immigrant students, Igoa (1995) found that in their childhood the young adults she studied experienced many problems in making the transition to schools in the United States. The most pronounced of these arose from associating with two cultures: How does one integrate two cultures in one person? One student described a feeling of being in exile upon arrival in this country. Another spoke of the differences between the two school systems and the difficulties in navigating between the system he knew and the one in which he needed to learn to work. These students also spoke of their period of silence and what that means: For one student, her silence was protection; for another it was a period of incubation leading to a higher level of adaptation; yet another observed the need for a "safe nest" to which she could retreat when she felt uncertain.

Diverse Views of Immigrant Education

Education is a tool of acculturation. It is important, therefore, to understand how U.S. government policies have shaped our official ideology concerning the education of immigrant students (Bailey, 1993; González, 1994; Lyons, 1990), and the function of the English language as an instrument of social control (Leibowitz, 1982). In general, government policy relative to the education of immigrant students has tended toward an assimilationist ideology. González (1994) has pointed out, as have others, that schools that align themselves with this ideology assume that the quality of education attained by immigrants depends on the degree to which they are quick to acquire the English language. In such a structure, non-English home languages are portrayed as a negative influence and a root cause of school-related problems for the immigrant young.

In this view, students from non-English-speaking cultures are deemed to be somewhat disadvantaged. Linguistic diversity is viewed with ambivalence at best, a temporary problem that is overcome when all students are able to function, in English, in mainstream education. In this most traditional of paradigms, the goal is English language learning as a means to acculturation and eventual assimilation. The imposition of this paradigm on schools shapes curriculum design and teachers' attitudes about immigrant and language minority students. It also affects how immigrant students are educated by lowering expectations for what they can achieve or by explaining their failure to learn as cultural failure on their part rather than as failure by the schools.

Alternative views and purposes are possible for the education of immigrant students. Among them are

- to prepare students to function professionally or vocationally in bilingual environments both here and abroad;
- to assert students' right to use their home language freely in and out of school;
- to develop in students healthy perceptions and feelings about themselves and help them succeed in school by providing a climate of respect for their home language and culture;
- to enhance their ability to participate effectively in the social, economic, and political processes of the society; and
- to reduce feelings of subservience of other language groups to English and reduce feelings of alienation from mainstream culture. (González, 1994)

Some of these views are friendlier toward diversity than others, and some are not strongly represented in the curricular repertoires of schools. Implicit in all of these views is the idea that there is value in maintaining the home languages of immigrant students, as there is value in learning English.

Professional development models that frame education for immigrant students solely in terms of deficit or remediation limit the scope of possibilities for the immigrant student and for the entire school community. Models that reflect broader rationales and that value diversity are more likely to develop in immigrant students the requisite skills and knowledge that will lead to full participation in the total school program. Such models provide opportunities for these students to develop English proficiency in community with their mainstream peers.

Because these models are not generally understood or embraced at district, state, or national policy levels, they are often excluded in discussions of policy development and in professional development for teachers and other school personnel. As older ideas of diversity are replaced by newer and more progressive views, it is important that professional development programs for teachers of immigrant students take into account the alternative conceptions outlined above for educating diverse populations. Professional development initiatives that include exploration of the instructional models corresponding to these alternative views will place the educator in a better position to choose the program design most compatible with the specific population in a given community.

Alternative models for educating immigrants offer special challenges to teachers whose attitudes and beliefs have been shaped by a view of immigrants that emphasizes an inability to speak English, a view based on deficits rather than assets. Teachers can and should explore the history behind this deficit view and clarify how it colors their instructional practice. From there it may be possible to examine other options more objectively. Professional development initiatives that include teacher reflections on their own attitudes and beliefs about diversity, both with reference to students and to themselves, can increase teachers' capacity to treat immigrant students as individuals, because teachers will understand themselves better, too (Calderón, 1995; Garman, 1986; Grant & Zeichner, 1984; Joyce & Showers, 1982, 1988; Wilsey & Killion, 1982). It is useful for teacher educators, or teachers themselves, to facilitate these discussions and reflections. In sum, better preparation for the teachers of immigrants suggests more than giving them a different toolbox. It is also necessary to examine the *meaning* of one toolbox as compared to others.

Government policies often influence the implementation of educational programs for immigrant students through allocation of special funding. This has profound implications for educators who are charged with the responsibility of educating immigrants. To promote understanding of what constitutes good practice, professional development efforts must include the critical study of education *policies*. They are no less important to teachers than are specialized skills in interacting with students.

Obstacles to Change

Because schools typically mirror the society they serve, changes in the local community influence interactions in its schools. However, certain factors inhibit the ability of schools to respond wisely to pressures to change. One such factor is the intransigence of traditional school structures and pedagogies. Another is the constraints imposed by external programs and regulations. A third is the nature of the workforce in schools, which may limit firsthand knowledge of the contexts in which students live. For instance, despite the fact that children of color represent a growing proportion of public school enrollments—from 28% in 1985 to 32% in 1995—most of the teaching force (86.5% in 1993–94) is White and not of recent immigrant origin (National Center for Education Statistics, 1997).

In addition to the changing demographics of schools in this country, the rapid pace of change in the workplace poses greater demands on schools. Whereas in previous generations there was room in the economy for newly arrived immigrants to fill low-skilled jobs (and the assumption was that each successive generation would have it easier), this circumstance no longer holds true for all immigrant groups (Berryman & Bailey, 1992; Carnevale, 1991; Chavez, 1994). The process of gradually increasing participation in this country's socioeconomic structures, which previously took two or three generations to accomplish, must now take place in one generation. Immigrant groups that lag behind in joining the economic mainstream risk falling into a cycle of poverty, dependence, and despair from which it is difficult to escape. This reality puts added pressures on school staff to find new ways of structuring instruction that allow immigrant students to integrate themselves into the school community as precursor to a similar integration beyond the school. In short, schools are expected to educate immigrants not only *better*, but also more efficiently than ever before.

In addition, some immigrant groups make their way into the American culture and polity with greater ease than others. This suggests that the nation's schools are capable of educating immigrant students quite successfully under certain conditions (Cummins, 1986; Nieto, 1991) and that interactional patterns in schools provide different experiences for different groups. Teachers, administrators, and policy makers need to understand why and how this occurs.

The challenges of this new context of complex diversity and urgency to succeed are made more complicated by the ongoing dynamics of school reform and restructuring that are taking place in many communities. New immigrants are arriving at a time when U.S. society is examining the very purpose and design of its schools. This includes a reexamination of the role of teachers. Many communities are enmeshed in changing schools in ways that are no less complex and diverse than are the new immigrant groups themselves. When the dust of these changes begins to settle, we may find that it is not enough for teachers to be better trained in the technical skills of teaching. This is necessary, but it is not sufficient. The teachers of today's immigrants, like the teachers of all other students, are called upon to participate in the redesign of the schools at the same time that they become more proficient in the art of teaching. It is a case, as one educator described it, of "changing a tire while the car is in motion."

Considered together, these factors point to the need for major changes in strategies for pre- and inservice teacher development. Professional development for teachers of immigrant students must include more than a mere exposure to the *artifacts* of the target groups (such as food, music, and dance). It must also include opportunities for teachers to examine their own *beliefs and ideas* about their relationships with immigrant people.

Lack of self-knowledge among educators can impede their ability to facilitate optimal educational experiences for immigrant students, but there are other obstacles as well. The hidden curriculum of schools transmits meanings such as what it means to work and to learn, the value of hierarchy and authority, what matters and what does not matter, and what it means to "be good" (González, 1993). There exists ample evidence that the hidden curriculum represents Eurocentric, middle class values (Anyon, 1980; Apple & King, 1983; Jackson, 1968/ 1983; Kohlberg, 1970/1983; Macdonald, 1981/1983; Vallance, 1973-74/ 1983), which are far from universal. Immigrant students who enter school with life experiences and languages that are different or exotic by traditional standards are thus at a disadvantage. Professional development opportunities for teachers of immigrant students must include examination of how teachers embrace, transmit, or transform the content of the hidden curriculum in instructional practice.

Teachers often are at a disadvantage when attempting to meet the needs of immigrant students, because they lack awareness of the mismatch between a student's experiences and the school's meaning (Lucas & Schecter, 1992; McIntosh, 1989). Teachers who lack an understanding of the variety of ways of perceiving themselves, their roles, and ways of being motivated to learn and achieve cannot apply sound principles grounded in that knowledge to their classrooms.

As language and culture play a critical role in classroom interactions, it is clear that immigrant students, whose language and culture may produce interactional patterns that are inconsistent with those of the school, have different school experiences than their mainstream peers. Immigrant students with preferences for learning in groups and demonstrating knowledge through exhibition, for instance, may encounter difficulties when attempting to function in institutional interactional patterns of the school as transmission-oriented pedagogy, instructional practices that consider students as vessels to be filled rather than creators of knowledge (Freire, 1970), and legitimization-oriented assessment tools, such as standardized tests (Cummins, 1986), especially when such devices are the sole measure of their progress. Factors such as tracking; standardized testing; curricula and pedagogy; the physical structure of the school building; disciplinary policies; and the roles of parents, teachers, and students in teaching and learning are so embedded in the fabric of school culture that school staff may be unaware of their potential effects.

Teachers and administrators who view cultural diversity as a problem or deficit, whose practices tend to exclude participation of community members and parents in the education of the child, whose pedagogy reflects a transmission-oriented approach, and whose assessment devices aim to legitimize the institution's judgment may discriminate unwittingly against students outside of the dominant culture (Cummins, 1986). Professional development that reframes the teachers' interpretations of immigrant students may provide a framework that helps reshape their curricular practices. The first lesson in this regard is that teaching is as much a cultural endeavor as it is the application of professional skills and knowledge.

Learning occurs when experiences build on learners' prior knowledge and experiences. Conflicts between the dominant culture of the school and that of the student disrupt the clarity of this relationship. When students are forced to devalue the cultural backgrounds of their families in favor of the prevailing culture of the school, learning opportunities are diminished. Those immigrant students who are able to navigate the differences between home and school cultures succeed; those who cannot may be placed at risk or subjected to remediation. The consequence of a mismatch between home and school cultures may be undue stress on the immigrant student's rate of acquisition of English, the most common social indicator of the acceptance of the core culture and its values.

Although there are many ways to teach English, most school staff yearn to discover "the best way." The pressure to utilize a single approach to promote English proficiency may place immigrant students with differing life experiences at a disadvantage. Professional development for teachers of immigrant students should include discussion of alternative approaches for the development of English language proficiency.

The convergence of these issues offers particular challenges to the professional development of educators who face more immigrant youth than before in their classrooms. Previously secure and predictable relationships between students and teachers may become uncomfortable or even dysfunctional as a result. Teachers and students may encounter difficulties understanding each other's languages and cultures mainly because they do not understand the role that language and culture play in school success. These misunderstandings may cause confusion and anxiety among the professional staff about immigrant students' ability to achieve the level of proficiency or knowledge that is necessary to compete successfully in school and in adulthood. Also discomfiting are the doubts experienced by many teachers over their failures to work successfully with all students and the lack of explanations concerning their failures. The unfortunate result for many teachers is the frustration of feeling not merely uncomfortable but also inept. Professional development experiences that offer teachers an opportunity to sort out their feelings associated with teaching immigrant students may facilitate their awareness of the factors contributing to their discomfort. One requirement for a new approach to professional development is that it be more reflective and more grounded in critical pedagogy than ever before. Another requirement is that district and school policies that may need to change to support more responsive pedagogy.

Given the demographic shifts in the student population and the relative constancy of traditional approaches to schooling by teachers who come from the mainstream culture, it is clear that the contemporary teacher must learn new skills, bodies of knowledge, and predispositions. These must be more closely aligned with the new culture that one encounters when students from increasingly diverse backgrounds converge in the school. Under these circumstances, teachers need new cognitive maps of what it means to teach effectively. They also need the background to be able to change their orientation toward the content and form of classwork in order to reach a culturally diverse student population. In the next section, we explore these skills, knowledge, and predispositions in greater detail.

An Emerging View of Effective Practice

What is it that teachers of immigrant students should know and be able to do? There is no single, simple answer to this question, but research provides some important understandings that can help develop effective classroom practices. Recent studies on the effective education of linguistically and culturally diverse students identify a number of teaching strategies, skills, and dispositions that teachers can learn, even if they are not specifically prepared as bilingual teachers (August & García, 1988; Carter & Chatfield, 1986; Cummins, 1986; García, 1989, 1993; Lucas, 1993; Lucas, Henze, & Donato, 1990; Moll, 1988; Pease-Alvarez, Espinoza, & García, 1991; Tikunoff, 1983). These include

• respect for and acknowledgment of the values and norms of the first language and home culture;

- ability to look carefully and objectively at students' various strengths and performances and build on those rather than focusing on English language skills as the primary factor in academic success;
- use of communicative patterns (rules of discourse governing ways of talking and working together in storytelling, question asking, and other interactions) that are consonant with those used in students' homes and communities;
- use of information and ideas from the students' own experiences and home cultures to promote engagement in instructional tasks and a feeling of belonging;
- encouragement and engineering of extensive peer interactions, including the creation of many natural communication situations;
- small heterogeneous and cooperative work group settings in which language can be practiced and feedback acquired around authentic learning tasks;
- encouragement for students to use their native language to share and acquire information during the course of their work, regardless of what language(s) the teachers use;
- focus on instructional content with attention to language development;
- modification of English communication approaches to match students' facility with English;
- communication by the teacher of high expectations for students;
- frequent, visible recognition of student success;
- expressions of caring for students and efforts to interact regularly with parents (through direct contact, school events and social settings, class newsletter, or other means);
- involvement of parents and community group members in the classroom and life of the school;
- use of multimodal teaching strategies that provide information through many avenues, including oral, written, pictorial, graphic, and kinesthetic;

- use of teaching techniques that are developmentally and cognitively appropriate, such as techniques that involve hands-on experiential learning, engage students in inquiry and testing of their ideas, allow for collaborative learning, and involve thematic instruction that integrates content and skills.

García (1993) summarizes several studies of effective classrooms for language minority students:

Effective classrooms recognize that academic learning has its roots in processes of social interaction. This type of instruction provides abundant and diverse opportunities for speaking, listening, reading, and writing along with native language scaffolding to help guide students through the learning process. A focus on social interaction encourages students to take risks, construct meaning, and seek reinterpretations of knowledge within compatible social contexts. Within this knowledge-driven curriculum, skills are tools for acquiring knowledge, not a fundamental target of teaching events. (p. 83)

Development of effective practices for immigrant youth can be enhanced by understandings of how people acquire and use language in cultural contexts; how adolescents grow, develop, and can be supported rather than impaired in their drive toward competence and autonomy; and how students' learning and understanding can be assessed through strategies that enable teachers to look and listen carefully and knowledgeably to what students are doing and saying.

Two notable illustrations of an application of this knowledge are content-based English as a second language (ESL) instruction and sheltered content instruction. Content-based ESL is the teaching of English through academic content as a means to help students develop conceptual and content knowledge at the same time they are learning English (see Brinton, Snow, & Wesche, 1989; Crandall, 1993; Mohan, 1986; Short, 1991). English language development includes the vocabulary and structures related to the content area(s) studied. These classes are often taught by ESL teachers who select content from one or more subject areas. Instruction is frequently provided through thematic units—for example, a theme such as Motion is chosen and studied from the prespective of several disciplines, including language arts, math, science, and social studies. Content-based ESL distinguishes between social and academic language. Social language may be acquired in 2 or 3 years. Academic language, the ability to communicate about academic tasks, requires more time (Collier, 1987; Ramírez, Yuen, & Ramey, 1991). In content-based ESL, the emphasis is on the acquisition of academic language.

In sheltered content classes, students study subjects taught in English by either ESL or content-area teachers (in most school districts, a certified content teacher must teach high school sheltered content courses for students to receive graduation credits). The classes are taught to meet the objectives for the content area set out for all students, but instruction is adapted so the language and content are accessible to students learning English. For example, teachers modify their language, use graphic organizers, and use multiple means (oral, aural, pictorial, and written) to help studens process information; they may focus on the main points of an issue rather than on all of the details; and there are many group hand-on activities and much class discussion. As with content-based ESL classes, these classes are usually composed entirely of English language learners. The teacher may or may not know the native languages of the students.

These approaches are supported by a number of theoretical principles. Krashen (1985) hypothesizes that a second language is internalized in two ways—through subconscious acquisition and conscious learning. Acquisition is similar to the way in which small children develop first and second languages through meaningful interaction in the language. Learning occurs through conscious attention to aspects of the language. Krashen's second hypothesis suggests that language structures are acquired when language input is comprehensible. Language can be understood even when it contains unfamiliar structures, if it occurs within a familiar context. The use of previous knowledge, context, and extralinguistic information are keys to understanding. This primary emphasis on acquisition of language in meaningful contexts is not to suggest that students at the secondary school level cannot profit from direct language instruction. They have language analysis abilities that can be brought to bear in their learning. However, formal instruction without significant meaningful contexts for acquisition and use is inadequate. Focus on language development alone, when students need to be learning academic content, is also inadequate. Motivation and relevance are important (Snow, Met, & Genesee, 1989). The use of relevant, high-interest material in instruction encourages student motivation, facilitates the learning of subject matter, and fuels language development.

Using the instructional strategies and ongoing diagnosis and assessment that are embedded in content-based ESL and sheltered content instruction requires a deep understanding of language learning and of different learning modes and strategies, so that teachers can make useful decisions about how learning can be supported. The teaching of human learning and development has been absent from many teacher education programs in the past. As a consequence, except when working with graduates of programs at the leading edge of teacher preparation, schools should assume that inservice professional development programs will need to address these areas of knowledge.

In reviewing research on classrooms that are effective for culturally and linguistically diverse students, García (1993) notes that common features undergirded the professional learning and teaching conditions available to teachers:

Classroom teachers … continued to be involved in professional development activities, including participation in small-group support networks; had a strong, demonstrated commitment to student-home communication (several teachers were using a weekly parent interaction format); and felt that they had the autonomy to create or change the instruction and curriculum in their classrooms, even if it did not meet with the exact district guidelines. … Principals tended to be highly articulate regarding the curriculum and instructional strategies undertaken in their schools. They were also highly supportive of their instructional staff, taking pride in their accomplishments. They reported their own specific support of teacher autonomy. (pp. 82-83)

García's findings reflect a view of professional development that focuses on "building a cadre of teachers and empowering them to engage in the rebuilding of their school, and working with the tensions and dilemmas that come as a result of making change" (Miller, 1992, p. 104). Such a strategy is essential to creating schools where equitable opportunities to learn and to teach are a paramount goal. Professional development that encourages teachers to create opportunities for inquiry for themselves as well as for their students improves the conditions of learning for everyone simultaneously.

Teaching is strengthened by structures, models, and practices that value community among groups and interpersonal collegiality within groups, cross-disciplinary cooperation that connects formerly fragmented curricula, and interagency collaboration with other social institutions within the community. These outreach efforts introduce new ideas to teaching and learning from formerly unavailable sources. The presentation of these new ideas in culturally diverse settings enriches the context and encourages the building of the beliefs, attitudes, and dispositions that accompany culturally responsive educational practice among competent, professional teachers.

Promising structural adjustments that enable these kinds of collaborations in schools and programs include

- organizing schools into "families" or "houses";
- providing a common planning period for teachers so they can work as teams to coordinate curricula;
- grouping students together for longer blocks of time;
- establishing a participatory governance structure among faculty and administrators;
- coordinating high school with adult education programs;
- allowing students to attend high school for more than 4 years; and
- offering classes at times when school is not normally in session.

(Lucas, 1993; Minicucci & Olsen, 1991)

Activities and services that can further support the education of language minority students are

- counseling, tutoring, and other support services;
- extracurricular activities;
- modified instructional approaches in mainstream classes that take into account language and cultural diversity;
- extensive support networks in the schools, districts, and communities and intentional efforts to ensure parental involvement with their children's education; and
- practices that reflect respect for language minority students' languages and cultures by learning about them, hiring bilingual staff from the students' backgrounds, and encouraging the use of the native language in school.

(Lucas, 1993)

In chapter 4, we describe the successful teaching and professional development practices of The International High School, a school for immigrant students in New York City. The practices at the school exhibit most of the educational and professional support features described in this research.

The structures and practices described above require educators with special skills and dispositions. Lucas's research (1993) indicates that such educators are knowledgeable about various aspects of education for language minority students and are involved in students' communities. They exhibit a commitment to serving language minority students and to the students themselves. The students in Igoa's study (1995) echo the need for a proactive stance, arguing that teachers of immigrant students need to understand the cultural and educational backgrounds of their students. They need to understand how the U.S. educational system discriminates against some students, and how they can help their students feel valued and accepted. Most of all, students want the teacher to be a role model and an "educational parent" whom they can trust and respect.

These informal comments from students, reinforced by other research findings, offer cause for reflection among teachers and administrators. They offer a starting point for planning new and more fruitful approaches to professional development for teachers of immigrant students. The traditional staff development model, which was focused on workshops and inservice courses, is of marginal use for the type of insights and proficiencies outlined in this chapter. The changes required to initiate and sustain new relationships with a more diverse student population are substantive. New and more complex arrangements for conducting this re-education of teachers—often by the teachers themselves—call for creative new ways of conceptualizing professional development. Some ideas for doing this are presented in chapter 2.

Concepts and Trends in Professional Development

The discourse on the education of immigrants often takes place apart from the national dialogue on school reform and restructuring. Arguably, this separate treatment can be somewhat beneficial, because it allows a more intense focus on the unique problems of the newly arrived. There is cause for concern, however, that as the national movement to restructure schools gathers momentum, the interests and needs of this growing segment of the population may be left unattended. The research coming from the arena of school reform has important implications for educating immigrants. Research in schools that are undergoing intense reform has underscored the need to reexamine the ways in which teachers learn about their profession and continue to improve after they have joined it. It seems clear that the issues of professional development that affect the teachers of immigrant children and youth are the same as those that affect other teachers, although they may be more complex because of the ways in which immigrants are welcomed (or not welcomed) into U.S. society. In this chapter, we review major trends in professional development for all teachers. In later chapters, we apply these concepts to the specific concerns of preparing and supporting teachers in educating immigrant youth.

Among the main themes flowing from contemporary research on school restructuring and professional development, we find the following: Teachers must become more empowered as professionals; they need to participate actively in how schools are run; they need a deeper understanding of the many ways there are to teach and to learn; they need to see themselves as partners with families and communities in the complex task of educating the total child, not merely the classroom child. Teachers are also being called upon to serve as architects in the design and construction of learning communities in which participants are both teachers and learners (Darling-Hammond, 1993). Yet because most teachers are not from the communities of the students they work with, do not share the languages and cultures of their students, and have had no specialized training in issues of language and culture, a variety of system changes are needed to ensure that teachers develop the knowledge they need and that schools develop supportive structures for empowering learning communities (Villegas, 1996).

The research on school reform is a clarion call to redefine what it will mean to be a teacher in the 21st century. Among the lessons of school reform is that teachers have a compelling need to become subjects rather than objects in the complex practices, structures, and politics of American education. This transition calls for a national dialogue designed to shift the emphasis in teacher education

- from teachers as passive recipients of information to active and engaged participants who produce their own knowledge and participate actively in charting their own professional growth;
- from teachers as seekers of a uniform method for teaching all children to active proponents of many ways of teaching and learning;
- from teachers with a technical orientation to their craft, in which they follow prescribed patterns, to a flexible orientation in which they make decisions about what works best;
- from teachers as carrying out a narrowly focused job of teaching students to multidirectional participants in converting schools into communities of learning;
- from teachers as rigid followers of instructional recipes to reflective practitioners who assess the meanings of their classroom activities and interactions on a continuing basis and can change their teaching methods to accommodate the needs of students; and
- from teachers as cultural agents who promote a hegemonic national culture to active participants in a movement to recognize and affirm cultural diversity in the nation.

These changes are important to all teachers, but they are more important for the teachers of immigrants, because the level of school efficacy with these students has greater consequences for the society. A poorly educated immigrant population is less likely to become integrated into the American mainstream. The schools are vanguard institutions in meeting this challenge.

The transformations envisioned in professional development for teachers suggest more than a willingness to adapt to the different world views that immigrant students may bring with them. They must include a reconsideration of old paradigms concerning what it means to teach and what it means to be educated. It may also be necessary to redefine the qualities that make teachers successful and to think anew about who should teach.

Traditional Assumptions Challenged

The problems and limitations inherent in traditional preservice education and in professional development models are well known to school staff. They are among the aspects of education that are in serious need of reform. Many teachers who prepared 15 or 20 years ago spent a modest amount of time learning basic techniques for teaching and little time learning about students, how they learn, or what they bring with them to school. In their inservice life, most teachers have experienced one or more sessions in which experts from outside the school present ideas, materials, or techniques in the manner of traveling salesmen. Teachers and administrators alike want to find ways to make organized growth experiences for teachers more meaningful and to eliminate the drudgery of ineffective sit-and-listen forms of inservice education.

Traditional programs of professional development, both inservice and preservice, have tended to emphasize the technical dimensions of teaching, an approach that often leads to intransigent notions about the one right way of teaching a given skill or understanding. This problem is deeply embedded in the traditions of U.S. schools, which regard teachers as technicians rather than as professionals (Clark & Meloy, 1990; Darling-Hammond, 1990) or as assembly line workers who are part of a grand, integrated curriculum scheme. Research suggests that staff training programs of this type are rarely viable as mechanisms to help teachers grow as critical intellectuals, as leaders in their schools and communities, or as effective participants in the redesign of the nation's system of education (McLaughlin, 1991).

The generally poor record of professional development activities appears to be rooted in a matrix of assumptions, misconceptions, and misplaced priorities. The most intransigent of these problems stem from a panoply of myths about staff development that many policy makers and practitioners accept as religious truths:

- that teachers resist new approaches because they lack information about new and better methods of teaching;
- that persons other than teachers are in the best position to determine what teachers need and to design teachers' professional growth experiences;
- that experts from outside the school constitute better resources than teachers themselves can be to each other, and that presentations by such experts are an effective way to help teachers modify and improve classroom practices;
- that listening is the best way for teachers to acquire new skills, and that having heard new ideas most teachers can integrate them into their own practice with little or no help;
- that workshops and presentations should involve as many teachers as possible in order to maximize their benefits district wide;
- that learning to teach is essentially a preservice activity, and that school district investments in professional growth should be modest (less than 0.5% in most districts);
- that most of what teachers need to learn is finite, static, and content-based; and
- that once teaching skills—authentic assessment, team teaching, methods of teaching English, etc.—are learned, they will rarely have to be relearned.

(Wood & Thompson, 1993, pp. 52-53)

These assumptions are highly questionable. Current research on teacher learning suggests that teacher development programs should focus on deepening teachers' understandings about the teaching/learning process and about the students they teach rather than on the implementation of new techniques, programs, or gadgets; must begin with preservice education; and must continue throughout a teacher's career. They must be collegial, inquiry-oriented, and connected to teachers' classroom work and to immediate problems of practice (Darling-Hammond, 1993; Lieberman, 1995; Little, 1993; McLaughlin, 1991).

Effective professional development activities move beyond the externally established, independent programs unconnected to school or classroom needs that have come to characterize teacher training. They reach beyond traditional professional, political, and bureaucratic boundaries to exploit the opportunities for learning that exist in teachers' work lives and in the communities of practice to which they connect both inside and outside the school. These kinds of teacher learning opportunities tend to be

- **experiential,** engaging teachers in concrete tasks of teaching, assessment, observation, and reflection that illuminate the processes of learning and development;
- **grounded in inquiry, reflection, and experimentation** that are participant-driven (i.e., learners take responsibility for posing questions and exploring answers);
- **collaborative and interactional,** involving a sharing of knowledge among educators;
- **derived from teachers' work with students;**
- **sustained, ongoing, and intensive,** supported by modeling, coaching, and collective problem solving around specific problems of practice;
- **connected to other aspects of school change and improvement.**

These approaches to professional development reflect a dramatic shift from old norms and models of teacher training and inservicing to new images of what, when, and how teachers learn. They focus, for example, on teachers' community of practice rather than on individual teachers; they reinforce norms of mutual assistance and collegial support, thereby challenging sink or swim workplace environments where every teacher is on his or her own. They move beyond a clinical supervision model of teacher education—whether preservice or inservice—

to foster strategies and skills of self and peer evaluation. These conceptions of professional development attempt to move beyond preoccupation with the present—on what just happened today or what will happen on Monday—to engage teachers in longer-term goals of inquiry, experimentation, and sustained change in classroom practice (Darling-Hammond & McLaughlin, 1995).

Wood and Thompson (1993) conclude that a new set of assumptions is needed for making structured professional growth experiences more meaningful for teachers. We review these proposed assumptions below, then integrate them with other emerging principles to create a conceptual foundation for new forms of professional development. While these ideas apply to most teachers, they are especially appropriate for teachers of immigrants, given the broader range of diversity they often encounter and the adverse teaching conditions they often face.

1. The school should be the prime focus for improving professional development practices tailored to fit the needs of teachers.

Current literature on adult teaching and learning does not encourage the use of large-scale staff development programs in which all teachers in a district are provided the same experiences. The assumption of the traditional design is that the needs of teachers at a given moment in time are comparable and that the same inservice event will be useful to all. We now know that this "one size fits all" approach does not benefit all teachers equally. To draw optimum benefits from structured growth experiences, teachers need to engage in experiences that are relevant to their unique school contexts and stages of professional development. This is the best reason for making the individual school the locus of professional growth interventions.

Schools that operate as communities are most likely to benefit from professional development interventions for teachers, because they often provide the best collegial support for changes in practice. It is at the school level that teams of teachers are engaged in experimentation and application of new ideas, knowledge, and skills. Because the same group of teachers participates in change over time, this approach highlights the lack of appropriateness of quick-fix presentations or a series of single-shot presentations by outside experts who are not part of the school team. However, teachers alone cannot change these approaches to professional development. Administrators and policy makers must also commit to these new designs, communicate the vision, and demonstrate leadership behaviors that support ongoing professional development (see, e.g., Miller, 1995).

Cross-school networks of teachers also have value. For example, teachers with similar student populations or content foci, such as middle school teachers of Russian-speaking immigrant students, could be grouped to participate in a professional growth experience. Participants in small grops focused on their scope of work feel more connected to the activities in which they engage and will continue to network and solve problems among themselves after a staff development event takes place.

It should be clear from this discussion that professional development must go beyond the use of lectures, a model that persists in most schools and university departments, including teacher education. Teachers need to have hands-on experiences in program and curriculum design, experimentation, and inquiry, along with knowledge about the theories that underlie their practices. Teachers should help to design their experiences within their own department, grade level, or school. They should also have access to growth activities that encourage communication and shared inquiry within networks of teachers. These activities should be supported at the district level as well as at the school (McLaughlin, 1991).

2. The goal of professional development is change. Meaningful change in educational practice takes considerable time, often as much as several years, to complete. Professional development programs may take a good deal of time to yield measurable results.

This is a powerful argument for a school-based model for planning and conducting professional development. If we regard professional growth as continuous, collegial, and long-term—as one aspect of the operant culture of the workplace—then experiences should be designed to engage teachers who can logically be expected to work together over a period of time. Most difficult problems encountered in matching the work styles of good teachers with the diverse needs of immigrant students require a long-term commitment to understanding what works with which students and under what conditions.

There are two realities with which we must contend: First, there is no guarantee that the methods that work with one group of students will work equally well with others. As immigrant groups change over time in a given school, and the needs of different groups of students emerge, the professional growth of teachers should allow for the development of multiple approaches to assessment and classroom interaction as well as for new kinds of knowledge. The second reality is that today's schools experience high levels of teacher turnover, and teacher cohorts may change substantially in a 5-year period. The factor of teacher mobility does not, however, negate the appropriateness of long-term plans for professional development; such plans are even more important in the context of mobility, because they provide a deliberative framework for new teachers and facilitate their entry into the school's unique context. Only in a long-term effort is it possible for teachers to understand fully that professional growth involves new thinking about the knowledge, skills, and predispositions they bring to classrooms. Only systematic practice and iteration, over time, can strengthen new ways of thinking about teaching and can cement that new thinking into changes in practice.

Contexts that have the capacity to build long-term commitments to professional development include teacher centers, peer review processes, teacher research, professional development schools, school-university partnerships, and teacher mentor programs. These contexts encourage the building of professionalism and professional growth by providing time for disciplined inquiry and encouraging colleagueship, openness, and trust. This leads to further networking activities both within and beyond the school's boundaries. When carried out in collaboration with teacher unions and other associations, this work can institutionalize an ethos among teachers that will support long-term commitments to change and professional growth (Lieberman & Miller, 1992; Schwartz, 1991).

3. Participation in professional development and selection of goals and strategies for professional growth should involve those who have a direct stake in the future of students—teachers, administrators, parents, community leaders, and the students themselves.

Teachers need to be involved in defining and shaping professional development opportunities so that programs are sensitive to problems of practice. Helping teachers and others identify their own development needs is a sensitive and difficult job for administrators and teacher leaders. It is as difficult and sensitive as doing performance appraisals or negotiating an agreement through collective bargaining. In the current age of shared leadership and decision making, the skills needed to guide these discussions and assessments are often subtle and delicate. The energies required to involve all those who have a stake are tremendous, but this is an important component for which plans must be made and resources allocated.

When language and cultural differences abound, it may be difficult to engage other stakeholders, such as parents and other members of the community. Their participation, however, is essential for the development of the consensual community that is necessary to define what kinds of professional development activities are needed to serve what purposes and to reach which goals. In some cases, the school-based needs may be more important or numerous; in others, the contextual needs of family or community may receive more resources or attention. There is no single pattern of problems and needs that are common to all communities.

Differences in language may make it difficult to involve immigrant parents in school-related decisions, and learning how to do so is an essential aspect of professional development. Some schools have discovered a benefit from involving parents: Developing family-focused education can be a means for entering into dialogue with immigrants and newcomers about the community's outlook on education and schooling (Moll & Greenberg, 1990). Parents can help to educate teachers about the values of and pressures on immigrant adolescents and the ways in which peer culture operates within their respective youth groups. Immigrant education is a context in which parents and teachers can truly learn much from each other.

Involving school support personnel in dialogues about the needs of students is also important. When secretaries, aides, custodians, and cafeteria workers participate in discussions with teachers, administrators, and parents, they can contribute important insights about the communities they are sometimes more a part of than are professional staff, and they can learn about ways their interactions with students can be helpful to the school's mission. These kinds of dailogues engender respect among school staff for each others' jobs and backgrounds and lay the groundwork for a collaborative school atmosphere.

School leaders and opinion shapers include senior teachers and other staff as well as principals and other administrators. In all cases, it is important that school leaders signal the importance of professional development by participating actively in it, by helping to shape it so that it is useful and rewarding, and by elevating its status in the culture of the school. It is important that school leaders participate actively in continuing education activities and not attempt to exempt themselves from participation. On the contrary, the literature suggests that administrators' participation is most clearly signaled by how they work to institutionalize professional development activities among teachers (Wasley, 1991). Professional development activities in which the entire school staff participate are critically important, because they provide an opportunity for more senior mentors to interact with less experienced teachers in a context of community. In settings where demographics have changed and new types of students attend the school, it is perhaps more important that the entire staff acknowledge the need to continue to develop their collective skills, abilities, and assumptions. The creation of a learning community is a major challenge.

4. Knowledge about adult learners should guide the planning and implementation of staff development activities.

It is an axiom of education that teachers tend to teach in the same ways they themselves were taught. Professional development programs are the logical venue for grappling with the evolution of teaching methods and principles. This is a delicate matter, however. Teaching young people is, or should be, different from the teaching of adults. Levels of background information, motivation, and collective ability to relate new knowledge and skills to previous knowledge and skills differ between K-12 learners and adult learners. The lessons of *andragogy*—the art and science of helping adults learn—can be helpful tools for designers of professional development programs. Andragogy offers the following clues about adult learners:

- Adults "have a deep psychological need to be generally self-directing, although they may be dependent in particular temporary situations."
- Adults draw from a larger reservoir of experience than do children and attach more meaning to those learnings that are drawn experientially.
- Adults are ready to learn something when they feel the need to know it.
- Adult learners "want to be able to apply whatever knowledge and skills they gain today to living more effectively tomorrow."

(Knowles, 1980, pp. 43-44)

It is also important to bear in mind that teachers often have age-related or experience-related patterns of development that are highly individual and idiosyncratic. This has implications for both program designers and teachers. For teachers to understand how the social context of their classrooms interact with the cultural background of their students, they must learn about these things in a context that recognizes their own developmental level as adults. For instance, the novice teacher may have the flexibility of time that may not be available to senior teachers. Senior teachers may be at a stage in life where investment in professional development activities competes with other personal and professional concerns that are a natural part of life for those in their second or third decade in the teaching profession. It is important for the teacher to recognize and reflect on how personal and professional circumstance may affect professional practice. Once recognized, it is possible to adjust for and correct unintended gaps in competence. In this context, professional development must accommodate these patterns while causing the participants to be reflective and critical about the life stages in which they are functioning and support teachers in making adjustments. Supports are critical for the teacher during those times of disequilibrium and frustration that accompany learning new and complex relational skills (Knowles, 1980; Oja, 1991).

5. Systemic support for change in professional practice is needed to sustain benefits over time. School and community leaders must make a commitment to providing the resources needed for schools to embrace and implement new outlooks, programs, and practices.

In almost every school district in the nation, professional development needs to be held in higher regard, as measured by budgetary allocations. The idea that teachers are prepared in college for eventualities that arise after they enter service must be discarded. Most teachers either do not receive extensive laboratory experience prior to obtaining a teaching credential, or their clinical teaching exercises take place in schools that are substantially different from those in which they teach after graduation (Zeichner, 1993). Often, too, the exigencies of completing degree requirements may overshadow the acquisition of knowledge, skills, and dispositions conducive to adaptive ways of teaching and managing classrooms.

Frequently, the demands of the school environment—especially in poor communities—are overwhelming to the young teachers who have not experienced them in their own lives. In those environments, young teachers may confuse the mechanics of effective crowd control with effective teaching. In frustration, they revert to the directive teaching methods of their own teachers, setting aside as irrelevant what they may have learned about more participatory teaching methods.

In many school districts, there are insufficient opportunities for teachers to take new ideas into the classroom, experiment with them, and discuss them with one or more colleagues to determine what elements worked best, with which students, and under what conditions. Too often, opportunities to discuss success or failure are not systematic. Teachers hear little encouragement to voice fears or insecurities and may fear being penalized if they do. This may be due to the perception that professional development is a remedial activity, carried out as a service to teachers who have been inadequately prepared or who are dated in their methods. Alternatively, it may be due to the bureaucratic conception of supervision as a summative exercise designed as a mechanism of social control over teachers and teaching. The conception persists in the minds of many administrators, even in good schools, that supervision is largely a control function rather than a tool for professional growth (Siens & Ebmeier, 1996).

Problems of inadequate design and die-hard traditions may be exacerbated by the budgetary limitations that plague school districts. Whether because of the forces of tradition, inadequate resources, or competing demands, little attention is paid to the effects that rapid changes in teaching goals, curriculum strategies, or student composition—such as an influx of immigrant students—may have on teachers who are expected to shift gears with little or no help or extra resources. Many administrators and school boards assume that teachers should have learned to teach *before* coming into the schools, hence, that continuing education activities are an unfair burden on schools, which have traditionally set aside limited resources for professional growth. This resentment toward the costs of continuing education for teachers and administrators makes it difficult to institutionalize these practices as a necessary and positive way of meeting the changing needs of schools, including changes in demography, technology, and skill sets needed for adult work.

It is inconsistent with the goal of the school as a learning community to deny the adult learners—teachers and other staff—full participation in the community of learning by limiting their access to professional development. In Lieberman and Miller's words, professional development "is about human development and learning for both students and teachers" (1992, p. 107).

A New Conceptual Frame

In the preceding section, we noted the limitations of many traditional models of pre- and inservice education with respect to their assumptions, design, organization, and support. In this section, we explore current conceptual and pedagogical changes concerning professional development. These changes go far beyond tinkering around the edges with the ways in which educators are now prepared, and they go beyond calls for new and badly needed financial resources. They involve changes in conceptions of teaching and teachers' roles; in conceptions of how teachers and students should interact; and in state and local policies and practices governing education, licensing, evaluation, and ongoing adult learning.

In a widely cited article entitled "Teachers' Professional Development in a Climate of Educational Reform," Judith Warren Little (1993) argues that the professional development of teachers is a critical element in the battle for education reform. According to Little, professional development is among the most rigid elements of the current structure of schooling in America and is in dire need of redesign. Without a serious look at this problem, there is little likelihood that serious, deep-rooted reform will gain a firm hold in many school districts.

If the crux of school reform is to create more flexible, adaptive classrooms and schools and to facilitate higher levels of performance for all students, then the key to success is preparing teachers who are knowledgeable diagnosticians and who use a wide range of strategies to meet the needs of diverse students (Darling-Hammond, 1990; González,

1993; Sykes, 1990). The challenge of redefining the role and function of teachers must be undertaken in tandem with efforts to redefine the knowledge and work of other educators and policymakers, including administrators, university faculty, and school board members (González & Szecsy, 1997).

The issues of professional development that attend the teachers of immigrants may appear to be unique, but they include the same issues that affect other teachers. For teachers of immigrants, the situation is made more complex by the attitudes of American society toward immigrants; the social, economic, and political results of those attitudes; and the evolving nature of education and teaching, which we discuss in the next section.

Preservice Education

In the past, because teaching was viewed as routine, semi-skilled work, many teachers were not well prepared to (1) develop curriculum and use teaching strategies grounded in a deep understanding of learning theory and knowledge of learning differences among diverse students; (2) critically evaluate students' progress and learning in light of knowledge of cognitive, social, linguistic, and psychological development; (3) create and use assessments that reveal student strengths, needs, and understanding; or (4) recognize the effects of cultural predispositions of students and teachers on their interactions with one another.

Giving teachers access to such knowledge is a major part of the transformation of teacher preparation and licensing that is on the horizon. It is also an important element of preparing prospective teachers so that they can be successful with the diverse range of students they are expected to teach. Supporting this success is critical to retaining teachers in the profession as well, since it will enhance the sense of efficacy that motivates ongoing commitment to the profession.

Unfortunately, most students in teacher education programs have typically had little or no experience working in low-income urban or rural schools where they are most likely to be hired, and little prior experience working with students with diverse learning needs (Zeichner, 1993). Teachers feel least well prepared in this area. For example, while the great majority of newly qualified teachers (84%) surveyed in 1991 felt adequately prepared to teach all of the subjects they were teaching, a much smaller number felt adequately prepared to teach the full range of diverse learners in their classrooms. Of those who taught native speakers of languages other than English, only 57% felt adequately prepared to do so. Of those who taught students requiring special education, only 60% felt adequately prepared (Gray et al., 1993). In another study, more than one in five preservice students reported that they were inadequately prepared to teach students with culturally diverse backgrounds, while reporting feeling much greater levels of competence in other areas (Howey & Zimpher, 1993). Clearly, here is an area where enhanced preparation could make a difference in new teacher effectiveness and, probably, continuation in the profession as well.

Over the last decade, many schools of education have made great strides in incorporating new understandings of teaching and learning in their curriculum for prospective teachers. More attention to learning theory, cognition, and learning strategies has accompanied a deepening appreciation for content pedagogy, constructivist teaching strategies, and multicultural perspectives. Explicit learning about the needs of diverse students, including English language learners, has been built into the teacher preparation curriculum in many schools of education.

In addition, teacher preparation and teacher induction programs are increasingly introducing strategies that help teachers develop a reflective and problem-oriented stance to teaching. This is done by engaging prospective teachers and interns in action research, school-based inquiry, and learning about students' experiences. In this way, prospective teachers build an empirical understanding of learners and a capacity to analyze and reflect on their practice. Steps are also being taken to deepen the awareness of prospective teachers about their role as carriers and disseminators of culture. This increases their understanding of the myriad ways in which they may be regarded by immigrant and minority students who differ culturally from themselves. We review several such programs in chapter 4.

A growing number of teacher education programs are inventing new structures for preservice teacher education that allow for a greater integration of theory and practice. Since the late 1980s, more than 200 professional development schools (PDSs) have been created as collaborative efforts that simultaneously restructure schools and colleges of education through teacher education programs co-constructed by university-based and school-based educators (Darling-Hammond, 1994a). PDSs create settings in which novices undertake student teaching or year-long internships in sites structured for state-of-the-art learning for both students and teachers. Professional development schools also provide sites for developing teaching knowledge by enabling practice-based research to be carried out collaboratively by new and veteran teachers, teacher educators, and researchers.

Unlike their counterparts in traditional teacher education programs, preservice teachers in PDSs complete an extended clinical experience that allows them to learn in a more structured cohort of student teachers with an organized faculty of veteran teachers and university-based faculty who plan curriculum together and co-construct seminars linked to the internship experience. Such an arrangement enriches the knowledge of the university-based and school-based teacher educators, as well. They often find themselves learning more about the theory and practice of teaching as they teach with one another and work with novices. For veteran teachers, watching someone else teach promotes reflection about teaching in general and about their own teaching. Novice teachers are socialized from the beginning into a collaborative culture, where collegiality and cross-disciplinary work are the foundation for their continued growth as educators.

Like teaching hospitals in the medical profession, professional development schools offer promise for supporting beginning teachers in developing state-of-the-art practice in settings that provide needed coaching and collaboration. Many of them are in urban schools that serve large numbers of immigrant and minority students. In these environments, new teachers not only receive ongoing evaluation and feedback from other teachers about their teaching, but they are also encouraged to participate in school decisions.

PDSs are true learning communities in that they offer opportunities for experimentation and mentoring in a sheltered environment where students are not test subjects, but rather part of a rich learning culture. Professional development schools aim to "educate all students to higher levels of performance, to accommodate and embrace diversity, and [to] ensure that all students learn to create, analyze, produce, adapt, and invent their own ideas and products" (Darling-Hammond, 1994a, p. 5). To achieve these goals requires teachers who understand learning and teaching, can address student needs as well as the demands of their content areas, and can mediate the gulf between students' experiences and curriculum goals.

Programs that develop teachers as managers of their own inquiry stand in contrast to earlier assumptions about teacher training: that beginning teachers need to focus only on the most rudimentary tasks of teaching, with basic precepts and cookbook rules to guide them, and that teachers in general should be the recipients and conveyors of knowledge, rather than generators of knowledge for and about themselves and their students. This passive conception of teaching and teacher learning is gradually being replaced. The function of teacher education is increasingly seen as a process of empowering teachers to develop, own, and use knowledge about teaching and learning in sophisticated ways. These new ideas are as powerful and demanding as the work of teaching requires.

Induction

It is generally agreed that there is a shortage of teachers able to meet the special needs of a growing language minority student population.

Once hired to work with this population—most of whom are immigrants—beginning teachers have often encountered challenges for which their preservice education did not prepare them. They experience a sink-or-swim situation that discourages them and leads many to leave the teaching profession. A major challenge of professional development work today is to compensate for this lack of preparation to face the cultural, attitudinal, and linguistic diversity that now prevails in many contemporary classrooms.

Stronger induction programs are needed to provide the necessary support that is so crucial for retaining new teachers and deepening their ability to meet students' needs, no matter how diverse these may be. In contrast to most other professions, which require structured, intensively supervised internships prior to licensing, teaching has traditionally offered prospective teachers little assistance in learning to teach, beyond a relatively short and idiosyncratic student teaching experience. Beginning teachers are generally left to learn by trial and error during their first years of teaching (Wise, Darling-Hammond, & Berry, 1987). Many of them leave; many others learn to cope, rather than to teach effectively.

Because the development of learner-centered practice is enormously difficult, untutored novice teachers often fail at their early attempts. The application of knowledge about learning, teaching, curriculum building, academic and language development, motivation, and behavior to the individual needs of diverse students is a daunting task. It requires skillful observation, diagnosis, and integration of many different concepts and abilities. Unless this occurs with the support of an able mentor, the effort can quickly become overwhelming. This is one of the reasons that knowledge acquired in preservice courses is often not put to use and that beginning teachers' practices often become less sensitive to students' needs, rather than more so, over the course of the initial year in teaching.

Teachers at all levels of experience agree on the importance of mentored induction. When asked in a recent survey what would have helped them in their first years of teaching, nearly all teachers called for more mentoring. Forty-seven percent felt that a skilled, experienced teacher who was assigned to provide advice and assistance would have helped substantially. Thirty-nine percent felt that more structured training, such as a year's internship before having their own classrooms, would have been most helpful (Harris & Associates, 1991). There is good evidence that mentoring programs improve beginning teachers' effectiveness and decrease attrition rates (Huling-Austin & Murphy, 1987; Odell, 1986; Wright, McKibbon, & Walton, 1987). Programs that have provided mentoring for beginning teachers in Los Angeles, New York, Cincinnati, Toledo, and Rochester have improved teacher competence, kept more teachers in the profession, and allowed for serious decisions about continuation and tenure. Torres-Guzmán and Goodwin (1995) reviewed this literature and found numerous studies where mentoring had beneficial effects. Such programs are especially important in the large cities and poor rural areas that have extraordinarily high attrition rates for new teachers (Cotton, 1987; Decker & Dedrick, 1989; Hersh, Stroot, & Snyder, 1993; Russell, Williams, & Gold, 1994). These include the five states in which more than 70% of immigrant students reside: New York, California, Texas, Illinois, and Florida.

The need for induction supports is obvious. Beginning teachers must develop the ability to apply knowledge appropriately in different contexts while responding to the many demands—cognitive, psychological, moral, and interpersonal—that simultaneously require attention in the classroom. Learning to manage the different personalities and needs of 25 or 30 students from many language and cultural backgrounds (and as many as 150 students in high schools), while prioritizing and juggling often-conflicting goals, does not happen quickly, automatically, or easily. These are skills that have to be developed over time. Too often there is a disjunction between the conceptions of good practice that beginning teachers learn in their preparation programs and those they encounter when they begin teaching. Typically, beginning teachers are placed in the most difficult schools—those with the highest rates of teacher turnover, large proportions of inexperienced staff, and the least capacity to support their growth and development. These are often schools where learner-centered practices are not well developed or well supported. In these settings, it is difficult for young teachers to develop ways of connecting what they know to what students know. The conditions for thoughtful, learner-centered teaching must be undergirded with expert, experienced staff who can provide guidance and instill confidence among new teachers.

An important part of the current redesign of teacher preparation and development includes new structures that extend the concept of mentoring in systematic ways, especially in schools that are undergoing significant change or are restructuring. A growing number of education schools are working with school systems to create internship sites, institutions like the professional development schools mentioned above, and other arrangements that allow new teachers to be inducted into schools as they must *become,* not only into schools as they *are.*

These internship and induction programs seek to enable teachers to learn first-hand about variability in students' development and approaches to learning while they are supported with guided instruction and opportunities for reflection on their teaching and its effects on learners. Seminars, opportunities for guided reflection, readings, and feedback tied to classroom work can be structured to help novices acquire wider repertoires of teaching strategies and to relate problems of teaching practice to research on teaching and human development. Having these kinds of opportunities available encourages beginners to teach reflectively, evaluate what they are doing, assess whether it is working and why, understand how to make better decisions, and juggle the many concerns of teaching. When these kinds of opportunities for learning to teach are provided in the early years of teaching, it is more likely that teachers will learn to attend to the unique needs of their students than adopt routines that are nonresponsive to the particular circumstances and experiences of the students they teach.

Ongoing Professional Development

The same issues that have emerged in preservice education also characterize changes in programs of ongoing professional development.
Among the emerging goals and assumptions for reform-oriented professional development are the following:

*1. Professional development programs should treat teachers as intellectuals
and change agents, helping them gain a stronger sense of professional
direction and efficacy.*

Among the most important understandings created by the current
school reform movement has been that fundamental changes must
take place in the ways that society, the profession, and teachers themselves look upon the teaching profession. There has been growing dis-
enchantment with the view of school systems as hierarchical organizations characterized by a policy-setting board, an executive superin-
tendent, and principals who function as plant managers supervising
teachers-as-workers. This arrangement—long considered the standard
paradigm in school administration—has become suspect, as education
analysts have learned the limitations of hierarchical organizational
schemes borrowed from the early years of assembly-line
manufacturing.

With the advent of site-based management, many schools have sought
to create environments in which teachers function as empowered professionals who participate in setting instructional and school policies.
These teachers are markedly different in outlook, performance, and
sense of accountability from work-a-day employees whose notion of
satisfactory work is following rules and regulations imposed by others.
The administrators who work with those teachers have also adopted a
more collegial and facilitating role, and they are prepared to share key
decisions about the mission and operation of the school. School boards
and superintendents must change their conceptions of their own jobs
as well as that of the teacher in order to achieve a realignment of roles

and responsibilities and a renewed sense of accountability on the part of the various role groups.

In the new conception of school organizations, the school is more like a living ecosystem than a factory. Its overall success is nurtured by a shared understanding of the interrelated and interdependent nature of the work that occurs within it. It operates best in a climate of professionalism and collegiality that borrows more from the professions than from the assembly-line culture of another age (Darling-Hammond, 1994a; Fullan, 1991; Sarason, 1982). An important goal of professional development programs is to enable teachers themselves to create a sense of accountability for teaching, the core function of the school. In order to institutionalize this new way of thinking about schools and teaching, teachers must learn to carry out their collective roles differently. Professional development programs, especially those involving cross-role groups, have a central role to play in this.

Some things will remain the same or will change only slightly. Teachers are also employees; many belong to collective bargaining units, and all are bound, to some extent, by rules and regulations from outside the school. It is difficult, in this climate, for some teachers to regard themselves as self-directed professionals possessing a sufficiently strong voice in charting the manner in which they will carry out their daily work. But the challenge to reinvent the profession is being embraced more broadly, as teachers and administrators gain greater comfort in performing work that is more reflective than prescriptive; more focused on the creation of independent learners than on the transmission of information; and more concerned with teaching the whole child than with covering the curriculum. To facilitate this transition, programs of professional development must be designed so that they exemplify to teachers how to move through the curriculum in a less linear and more creative fashion. Concepts are emerging within and outside of the teaching profession—for example, hypertext, cognitive mapping, and conceptual scaffolding—that offer guidance on the new set of skills that must be mastered. All three provide means of making connections and drawing relationships.

Hypertext, here portrayed as a concept, involves accessing and organizing information into knowledge through other than linear relationships. Using hypertextually organized information permits teachers and other school leaders to make meaningful linkages between concepts in a way that is more difficult in traditional, linearly arranged information banks. In a hypertextually arranged learning environment, teachers are not bound by linear conventions, such as discrete fields of information, that frequently militate against building cross-disciplinary relationships, and can build a more broadly based knowledge bank about professional practice (González & Szecsy, 1997).

Cognitive maps are symbolic representations of knowledge about the social context. For instance, drawing Venn diagrams that represent the relationship between knowledge and beliefs (Alexander & Dochy, 1995) or between diversity and community (Szecsy, 1996) is a way of illustrating an individual's knowledge about these abstract concepts. Representing concepts graphically and explaining the graphic representation in a social context can provide participants in such exercises with the opportunity to bring their own insights to consciousness and to hear the insights of their colleagues in a nonthreatening environment. Cognitive maps provide a mirror into which teachers and administrators can look in examining their ideas about their environment.

Conceptual scaffolding is the process of a facilitator providing a framework onto which professionals can hang supporting details specific to their environment. For example, in the context of an informal conversation, a researcher could present knowledge about exemplary teaching practice in other places. Gradually, participants make heuristic discoveries about what they hear and connect it with what they do in practice. Reflecting on the gap between the two provides school staff with the cognitive space in which to construct new knowledge that will fill the gap with locally appropriate interventions.

Emerging research is beginning to indicate the utility of combining these concepts for the design of new ongoing professional development activities, including indications that the act of research is itself a professional development activity (Wasser & Bresler, 1996). The combination of hypertextual information, cognitive mapping, and conceptual scaffolding supports teachers as they seek to understand themselves and the complexities of their environment better. These tools also help school staff explain the interaction between beliefs or interpretations about diversity and professional practice (Szecsy, 1996). All of these tools give teachers an opportunity to engage in dialogue with each other; to reflect actively on their thoughts and ideas about language diversity; and, in the supportive environment of a collegial community, to draw their own insights—including some uncomfortable realizations—about their own practice in the context of diversity. Once these thoughts, ideas, and feelings are articulated by the teachers themselves, it is possible for facilitators to guide them in their professional growth. This approach places faith in the professional's inherent intelligence and desire to provide what is good for instruction of immigrant students.

2. Teachers must be involved in professional development decisions.

It has become common for school critics to proffer a deficit model of teachers, which assumes that they are comfortable with what they do and oblivious or hostile to better ways of teaching. In some cases, this may be true; traditions tend to produce a certain level of comfort and become self-perpetuating. But in most cases, a different condition exists. For many teachers, a reluctance to work differently is not grounded in resistance to change or in excessive attachment to tradition, but rather in a conviction that they are doing their best and that the practices they use have been effective with (other) students in the past.

To be faced suddenly one year with an intractable problem that used to be only mildly challenging can be unnerving. This can happen to teachers—and to other professionals—when major changes occur in student populations and greater diversity results. The sense of self-efficacy is shaken, and the result is often a binary choice: an openness to new and perhaps untried ideas or, more often, a tendency to blame the students for refusing to learn what others have been able to learn before in response to the same teaching. This blame then shifts to other areas as well: to immigration policies, poor home environment, lack of parental interest in education, an unwillingness by the student to learn English, and so forth.

When teachers are not involved in analyzing dysfunctions and designing their own programs of professional growth to address the situation, a choice is removed. Remedial, compensatory programs of improvement are prescribed, and the underlying problem remains hidden. Teachers are left to wonder to what degree the problem is their own practice and to what degree sociocultural or economic factors are the source. When a decision is made to remediate teachers—no matter how well informed that decision may be—they are deprived of the opportunity to act professionally and are pushed back into a technical position that calls for diagnosis and prescription to be made elsewhere, by persons other than the teachers themselves. The result of this is a form of professional disempowerment, because the choice has been made *for them* rather than *by them*.

When teachers and other school personnel are denied the opportunity to examine in an intellectually rigorous way the dilemma that faces them, it is difficult for them to accept the diagnosis that must inevitably follow, explicitly or otherwise: that they are deficient and must submit to some form of professional remediation. A difficult situation thus becomes harder to understand and accept. When teachers are simply told what they must do and not allowed to reach a conclusion based on their own study of the problem, they are precluded from using new knowledge, deliberation, reflection, and self-correction, the most important aspects of any profession and any change process.

In the generalized criticism of the teaching profession, critics often forget that teachers are not unlike other professionals: All things being equal, they would prefer to do a good job than a poor one. Differences in teacher willingness to commit to structured professional growth in a climate of change may be attributable to many factors. Among the most important of these are the degree to which they have been effective in the past, the degree to which they participate in articulating their own professional needs, and the degree to which they help to identify ways of addressing new professional challenges. For some, it may help to visit classrooms similar to their own and to observe other teachers at work. For others, it may be useful to have a formal review of teaching and learning theory. For still others, ongoing conversations with other practicing colleagues may be useful. All of these activities can be part of a successful program of professional development. The degree of ownership and legitimacy afforded to various practices is most likely to be higher when the teachers themselves participate in weighing their relative value, as opposed to having them imposed as a part of a regimen of enforced retraining.

3. New structures for individual and organizational learning must replace notions of "inservice training" or "dissemination" with possibilities for knowledge building and sharing focused on team approaches to problems of practice.

To serve teachers' needs, professional development programs must provide a range of opportunities that allow teachers and others to share with each other what they know and what they want to learn, and to connect their learning needs to the context of their own teaching environment. Professional development activities must allow teachers to engage actively in experiences with other teachers that are sustained over time and that allow them to reflect on the process as well as the content of what they learn. This is especially true in the case of teachers of immigrants, some of whom may have special knowledge and expertise in areas such as ESL or valuable firsthand understanding of students' cultural backgrounds. Such complementary sets of skills and knowledge can be readily shared among teachers, when sharing is given institutional legitimacy as part of a professional development program. Taken together, the bringing together of skills from many teachers yields a situation where the whole—what each one gets from all the others—is greater than the sum of the parts.

The key structures are those that break down isolation, empower teachers with high-level professional tasks, and provide opportunities for thinking through new approaches to practice. They range from professional networks that operate across school district lines to more collaborative professional roles and learning opportunities within schools that can take many different forms. In all of these, the struggle is to reduce the significance of artificial boundaries and borders such as departments, grade levels, schools, and even school districts. Opportunities to be professional should not be constrained by the artificial boundaries established to facilitate school management and governance.

The organizational side of the lives of teachers often receives as little attention as the intellectual side. Teachers, more than other professionals, must learn to function in groups, to be consultative and collaborative, and to seek communal tasks and events with which they can create a distinctive school culture. Unfortunately, there are few opportunities for teachers to learn this aspect of their work lives. The old adage that teachers reign over their classrooms once the door is closed is an indicator of the ways in which schools are structured for isolation, and teachers come to view themselves as masters of a small universe rather than as collaborators in a larger, school-wide project.

Peter Drucker (1989) has noted that the hallmark of the end-of-century "knowledge worker" is collaborative work and joint effort, rather than independent work. The effectiveness of knowledge workers, Drucker asserts, rises or falls, depending on their ability to work closely with others. Although they are often unaware of the loss, modern organizations lose productivity when they undervalue group work. According to Drucker, the efficiency of the modern-day knowledge worker—which includes virtually all professionals and others who work with information rather than objects—is jeopardized by a reclusive attitude toward work. This is no less true for teachers than for anyone else. Because collaborative teaching has been so rare in schools, teachers need intensive and extensive practice in forming and optimizing collaborative work arrangements.

4. A school culture supportive of improved practice and professional growth is essential to successful programs of professional development.

The vagaries of school culture are often difficult to pinpoint, but school staffs usually agree that schools, like all workplaces, have a collective attitude concerning staff learning and inservice education. In some cases, teachers may look upon inservice education as burdensome extra work inflicted on overworked and underpaid teachers, or as a form of compensatory education imposed by administrators who regard their work as inadequate. Inservice sessions may range from open, effusive, and collegial events with much sharing of ideas and excited interaction to somber, uncomfortable events in which the participants sit with arms folded across the chest waiting for the clock to spell relief.

What are the causes or conditions behind these variations? The success of any program of professional growth is commensurate with how much the participants embrace it as their own, how much they are allowed to plan for it, and how much it is drawn from their own needs and interests. It is in this way that professional development becomes an integral part of the school's collective attitude of continued improvement. Senge (1990) and others describe the ideal culture of a learning organization as one in which all persons in the organization are learning at the same time they are teaching. Professional growth takes place when school staff live out a conviction that growth and learning are expected not only from students but from everyone else in the school, that it is enriching rather than remedial, and that it is the core work of the organization.

5. An integrative view of professional growth must be grown at the level of the local school. School-based professional development and site-based management are tightly bound, integral components of school-based improvement.

Professional development programs must be regarded as essential elements in school district budgets. To make this happen, planners should ensure that these programs include components for school improvement along with a continuing emphasis on individual and collective professional growth for teachers. It is not uncommon for administrators and policy makers to discuss school-based management, school-based decision making, and school-based budgeting as a unitary package of ideas and procedures connected to reform. It is less common to see professional development efforts included in the same discussion. This compartmentalization and segregation of functional activity is regrettable. It separates the primary function of schools (to teach the young) from their administrative support functions (the management of personnel and other resources), often placing more stress on the latter than on the former. In the process, the sense of priority and focus may be lost or misplaced. How decisions are made and how funds are used are part and parcel of how schools succeed in carrying out their central mission. How well staff are prepared is clearly no less important. Only a continued stress on the primacy of the teaching function can assure that the mission will remain paramount.

6. It is vitally important to prepare teachers to be thoughtful, reflective professionals with strong intellectual roots as well as technical skills.

Judith Little (1993) suggests the following:

The well-tested models of skill development, built on the staff development and implementation-of-innovations literatures, will work reasonably well to introduce those aspects of reform that are "technical," or can be rendered as a repertoire of classroom practices. ... We know how to do training well, and could probably do more of it well but the training paradigm, no matter how well executed, will not enable us to realize the reform agendas; and resource allocations for professional development represent a relatively poor fit with the intellectual, organizational and social requirements of the most ambitious reform efforts. (p. 5)

The intellectual side of teaching—the building of reflective and ethical practice—is often given short shrift in continuing education programs for teachers. In an era when a "world class education" refers primarily to job preparation and international competitiveness in labor markets, there is less room for the contemplative side of education and for examining its function as a basis for reflecting on the human condition.

The stress on accountability, outcomes, and performance often translates into pressure for measurable teacher competencies, to the detriment of less measurable qualities of intellectual inquiry or creativity. Among the many ways this is reflected in teacher education is the popularity of workshops on test-taking skills and the use of standardized test scores as measures of effectiveness. Too much emphasis on short-term gains can cause erosion in the foundations on which long-term successes are built. Teachers of immigrant youth need to give attention also to the history, intellectual traditions, and heritage of their students and how these shape their ways of perceiving and behaving.

In short, the intellectual side of teaching must receive greater emphasis in professional development programs, and accountability demands must be balanced against the need to understand the cultural differences of students as expressed in the arts and humanities. For example, explicit instruction in classroom techniques for teaching English must be balanced with knowledge about readings that students may be doing in their home language and ways that public media such as television can be harnessed to help develop language skills outside the classroom.

Whether or not they participate in a formal program of bilingual education, teachers should know how to use reading resources in the home languages of their students to facilitate students' acquisition of knowledge and information. We need to remind ourselves of the obvious: Most knowledge and information can be learned in any language, and reading in all languages is good. In many communities, the Spanish language, for example, is an important linguistic resource often ignored by schools in their haste to teach English (González, 1994). There are more speakers of Spanish in the United States than there are speakers of all other non-English languages combined. As the nation's second most important language, Spanish has a special potential—not shared by other small-group languages—to serve as a link between schools and communities on a large scale.

The intellectual base for teaching is many-faceted. A climate rich with sustained and relevant opportunities for teachers' learning resembles a web, where networks, seminars, and reading and study groups crisscross one another, providing an array of in-school and extra-school opportunities for teachers to pursue their interests. Occasions for teachers' continuous intellectual renewal must be multiple and diverse, rather than generic and self-contained, if they are to be responsive to specific content-based or learner-based concerns.

Effective professional development activities similarly are fluid and have various life cycles. The focus of policy concern should be on the quality of teachers' general environment in terms of opportunities to learn. The richness of the overall menu is what matters.

However, none of the above will matter much if teachers feel it is not safe to admit mistakes, to try and possibly fail, or to disclose aspects of their teaching where they feel inadequately prepared or uninformed. As a venue for problem-solving, self-evaluation, and experimentation, professional development activities require trust and a sense of personal and professional security. An essential role for leadership involves establishing a climate of trust and a habit of problem solving rather than problem hiding. In the next chapter, we discuss how communities for real learning can be created.

Structures, Models, and Practices in Professional Development

In this chapter, we discuss ways in which traditional instructional practices and the design of staff development experiences are evolving to increase their effectiveness in an era of school change and restructuring. We outline emergent forms and structures for professional development that aim at changing schools' conceptions of the nature of education and the cultural matrix in which schools operate. Finally, we examine the professional development models, structures, and practices that permit teachers to use constructivist instructional strategies to meet those needs.

Promoting Community and Collegiality

We discussed earlier how traditional staff development workshops often limit the amount and quality of professional communication among practitioners. The limitations that such forms of staff development place on critical discussion and analysis impede teachers' adoption of new attitudes, beliefs, and dispositions about immigrant students and their understanding of the need to change the ways they work. Both cross-school and within-school strategies for professional development, as well as work in preservice education, are creating greater possibilities for critical discourse and analysis of practice. These strategies help to create professional communities that inquire together about changes in practice and in-school opportunities for enacting these changes with collegial supports.

Professional Communities and Partnerships Outside the School

Recent restructuring initiatives in many communities have shown that a powerful form of teacher learning comes from participating in "professional communities" that extend beyond their own school buildings (Darling-Hammond & McLaughlin, 1995). These communities can be organized across subject-matter lines, around significant pedagogical issues, to enhance school–community relations, or in support of particular school reforms. They are valuable because they legitimate dialogue and support the risk taking that is part of any process of change. Vehicles for developing such communities include

School–university collaborations engaged in curriculum development, change efforts, or research. When such relationships emerge as true partnerships, they can create new, more powerful kinds of knowledge about teaching and schooling, as the "rub between theory and practice" (Miller & Silvernail, 1994, p. 44) produces more practical, contextualized theory and more theoretically grounded, broadly informed practice.

Teacher-to-teacher and school-to-school networks. They provide "critical friends" (Costa & Kallick, 1993, p. 49) to examine and reflect on teaching, and opportunities to share experiences and to develop new practices or structures. The National Writing Project and the Urban Mathematics Collaboratives are examples of such teacher-to-teacher networks. They are powerful learning environments because they allow people to engage in collective work on authentic problems that emerge in their own efforts, get beyond the dynamics of their own schools and classrooms to encounter other possibilities, and experience and solve similar problems (Lieberman & McLaughlin, 1992; Little & McLaughlin, 1991).

Partnerships with neighborhood-based youth organizations such as club programs, theater groups, literacy projects, museums, or sports groups. They provide teachers with important and sometimes otherwise-unavailable information about their students' homes and neighborhood settings, insight into students' nonschool interests and accomplishments, and opportunities for coordination between school and youth organization activities to promote students' learning. In the case of immigrant and minority students, of relationships with ethnic organizations have the added advantage of helping teachers understand the dynamics of day-to-day life in the students' communities and gain useful information about the social systems of which their students are a part.

These new communities of practice involve new actors and new agencies in teachers' learning and growth. They depart from traditional notions of institutional relationships, which assume that teaching is shaped and structured primarily by school systems. These extra-school structures and supports represent a broader, more expansive, and more inclusive profession that values partnerships on behalf of children and youth. Their concerns extend beyond maintaining institutions to deepening the capacity of educators to serve their students and the capacity of the profession as a whole to advance knowledge.

Learning Communities Inside the School

Inside schools, teachers' schedules, habits, and professional cultures must foster critical inquiry into practices and student outcomes. Inquiry is the nucleus of true communities of practice in which teachers meet together to solve problems, consider new ideas, evaluate alternatives, and frame school-wide goals and initiatives. Specific activities that promote such discourse and learning include

- teacher-initiated research and school-based inquiry;
- peer reviews of practice; and
- team teaching and joint curriculum work.

All of these processes provide opportunities for teachers to examine practice collectively and without the pressure of evaluative procedures that are part of school governance. As teachers become engaged in looking purposefully at their work, their students' work, and the work of colleagues, they plumb more deeply the many facets and aspects of teaching and learning.

Peer review of practice can occur in many ways: as faculty collectively examine aspects of their curriculum or other practices, as they look at particular concerns within the school, as they develop and participate in peer evaluation and peer coaching activities, and as they participate in assessments of students. Teacher engagement in assessments of teaching and learning is proving to be a powerful tool for learning.

Collective teacher engagement in assessing student work, for example, deepens teachers' understanding of learning and can be a powerful lever for both pedagogical and organizational change. When teachers and schools take on the challenge of developing authentic, multifaceted assessments of student learning, they begin to look at how students learn as well as what they know, and to identify areas of strength as well as areas of need. Authentic assessment strategies have been found particularly successful with students who are new English language learners because they provide information to teachers about these students and varied opportunities for students to demonstrate their knowledge and skills (Darling-Hammond, Ancess, & Falk, 1995; Falk, Macmurdy, & Darling-Hammond, 1995). In the case of immigrant students, these reflective deliberations among teachers can help them get a clearer picture of language and cultural conflicts that may exist in the school community and encourage them to address such problems in a constructive manner.

Critical professional analysis of this type can become the basis for transformative learning that enables teachers to change their paradigms of what schools and teaching might look like and accomplish. Similarly, teachers who have engaged in effective forms of teacher assessment, such as the year-long reflection and documentation they undertake in building a portfolio for the National Board for Professional Teaching Standards, claim they have learned more through this process than in any other staff development activity (Cascio, 1995; Darling-Hammond, 1994b). Looking closely at authentic work—one's own or someone else's—through a lens that is built on a powerful conception of teaching yields a clear understanding of teaching and learning and stimulates professional growth.

The need for collaborative inquiry and learning exists for other educators as well, including school principals, teacher directors, and community leaders involved in education. The same is true of other support staff, such as school psychologists, counselors, and teacher aides. These staff should be included, as much as possible, in in-school and out-of-school activities to examine teaching practice and learner outcomes. Cross-role participation in professional development activities has been found to be more productive in stimulating shared understandings of school goals and new approaches than are activities that treat teachers, principals, counselors, and others as separate groups for whom different conversations and topics are relevant (Fullan, 1991). For example, extended institutes for school-based teams of teachers, administrators, and parents have proved to be critical for launching school reforms in cities like Hammond, Indiana, and Louisville, Kentucky (Lieberman, 1995). Participation of counselors, school psychologists, and parents as well as teachers and principals in shared development activities is central to successful change. Professional development for all members of the school community contributes to a common sense of purpose and practice rather than reinforcing the separations that already exist.

Cooperative learning

Cooperative learning is a practice where learners are organized to work in mutually supportive work groups. Originally developed in linguistically homogeneous settings in which there were few language minority students, cooperative learning methodologies are increasingly used in language-diverse classrooms. A hallmark of this approach to learning is cooperative learning structures, "content-free ways of organizing social interaction in the classroom" (Kagan, 1993, p. 9). These are distinguished from activities that are bound to content. Cooperative learning structures draw from the complementary knowledge and talents of learners and integrate them synergistically, so that the sum of the collective group knowledge exceeds its individual components. Cooperative learning structures facilitate team building, communication building, content mastery, concept development, and other multifunctional and interactional concepts. Because interaction is a major feature of cooperative learning, language minority students benefit from increased contact and richer experiences with language, both their home languages and English.

Just as educators learn more deeply in professional communities, so do students. In traditional classrooms, it is not uncommon for teachers to talk more than their students. Further, traditional views of schooling often assume a common orientation by students to the content of instruction. However, attitudes and predispositions may not be universal among all students in the world; hence, some immigrant students may not share them or may share them to a different degree. Traditional pedagogy also limits the development of immigrant students' communication skills, because it limits opportunities for them to use language in authentic contexts.

Cooperative learning offers opportunities to merge the social integration needs of immigrant youth with new ways of organizing learning and teaching. Cooperative learning builds on the social nature of learning. Because it regards classmates as teaching resources, it is an excellent vehicle for providing immigrant students with an authentic context in which to improve their capacities to communicate in English on topics that may be more useful and interesting to students than subjects in the prescribed curriculum.

Helping teachers learn about cooperative learning by using cooperative learning strategies in professional development can strengthen teachers' academic, pedagogical, and social skills in educating immigrants. Showing teachers how cooperative learning helps them to learn facilitates their use of these methods in helping their students to learn. Experiencing high-quality cooperative learning with diverse colleages, and learning how to manage high-quality cooperative learning with diverse students, may also help teachers to reduce their tendency to look upon cultural and linguistic differences as negative traits that impede teaching and learning.

Encouraging teachers to engage in their own forms of cooperative learning encourages reflection about their craft. It may improve their sense of efficacy and respect for learner differences by putting them in a learning role that is similar to that of their new students. Through its use as a tool for professional development, cooperative learning encourages teachers to regard the school as a learning community of students and teachers engaged in multidirectional interaction and learning, rather than a one-way transmission setting in which teachers dispense and students absorb information and knowledge.

The use of group learning strategies in professional development can build a sense of community among educators in culturally diverse settings and enable teachers to develop personal resources and competence in using them (Mosher & Purpel, 1972). Of special interest to teachers of immigrant children and youth is the efficacy of this approach for developing teacher awareness of multiple perspectives and a variety of approaches to problem solving. The skill of framing and reframing problems until they are amenable to solution is extremely useful to teachers. In addition to demonstrating how learning styles may differ in a given group of students, group learning reduces the likelihood that teachers will fall into unproductive problem-solving and decision-making patterns that are heavily laden with cultural symbols unfamiliar to immigrant students. Once trust and confidence are established, being in community with others encourages risk taking among teachers, empowering them to work at integrating new practices into their repertoire. When teachers themselves experience the dynamics of group learning, they are better able to understand how English language communication skills can be encouraged among immigrant students through genuine practice and exposure to the rich array of English language voices of their peers.

Problem-based inquiry

Sometimes teachers are at a disadvantage when attempting to interact with immigrant students, because they lack the knowledge to utilize practices that are sensitive to the array of learning preferences that may be present in their culturally diverse classrooms. Professional development strategies such as problem-based inquiry and teacher-generated curriculum work (Miller, 1992) allow teachers to focus on immediate problems of practice relevant to the students they serve. Action research, where staff development is organized around a problem in practice, is a common form of problem-based inquiry. In action research, teachers identify a problem for study, read research literature, design an intervention, collect data, and evaluate their findings. For example, teachers may want to find out what adults do to facilitate immigrant students' developmental, academic, cultural, social, and linguistic transitions in a middle school setting. Their research might report on their observations. The cycle repeats itself throughout the teacher's career. Alternating periods of study and reflection occur throughout the process.

A companion of problem-based inquiry is teacher-generated curriculum, because out of teacher-initiated inquiry will come teacher-generated ideas about curriculum that can better serve the characteristics of immigrant students. Returning to our example, teachers may elect to write curricular interventions that address immigrant students' transitions at the middle school level through the use of technology supports (Macdonald & Szecsy, 1996). The curriculum project becomes the intervention from which teacher research can be based and teachers' instructional practices informed. Thus, teacher-generated curriculum is one professional development strategy that can support instructional strategies that are culturally responsive.

Teacher-generated curriculum has the following characteristics (Miller, 1992, pp. 105-106):

- Teachers work together as colleagues; they pool knowledge and resources; they work on collective enterprises.
- Professional knowledge develops from understandings about the craft of teaching, based on experience and practice.
- Teachers are decision makers about professional practice. Instructional leadership is the purview of teachers.

Thus, teacher-generated curriculum counters the deficit-training model of staff development. In this respect it corresponds more closely to the cooperative learning and authentic assessment strategies advocated for classroom instruction for students.

Coaching strategies

Many experts recommend that professional development be an integral part of daily life in schools. They argue that staff development initiatives relegated to summer vacation periods and at the end of busy school days will be of limited effect because of the distance between the staff development activity and the place where the objectives will actually play out—in classrooms with students (Joyce & Showers, 1982, 1988).

Peer coaching as a vehicle for ongoing inquiry into practice is increasingly being adapted by schools. It includes study of current practice, demonstration of exemplary practice by collaborating teachers in the context of a learning community, and feedback from peers who are also involved in the process. Among the purposes served by peer coaching are the establishment of a professional and supportive structure that expands teachers' repertoires, breeds collegiality, and infuses new knowledge into instructional practice. This is especially important in culturally diverse settings where students represent a broad range of learning styles.

For teachers of immigrant students, peer coaching can begin with the study of the theory and rationale behind multicultural education and of language acquisition, development, and use in mixed cultural contexts. This would include reading books and articles that discuss these topics, discussing the readings and teachers' own experiences in light of them, observing demonstrations by master teachers of strategies relevant to these topics, practicing these strategies in classrooms, and obtaining feedback from colleagues. Training in the art of observation and feedback can occur simultaneously with the introduction of an instructional innovation. While new practices are being tried, teachers may convene as a group to talk about problems and progress related to their in-class use of the ideas and to examine instructional objectives, syllabi, materials, and texts in light of the new teaching strategies. In individual conferences, observers serving as coaches can raise particular issues that arise in individual classrooms. In classrooms with immigrant and minority students, the particular issues raised by language and culture should receive special attention. The role of the teacher-as-coach is twofold: He or she can assist the observed teacher in seeing the material from the vantage point of students, bringing to consciousness the taken-for-granted patterns of language and behavior that students use and that the teacher uses in response. In addition, a teacher coach can help the observed teacher examine these patterns and other teaching choices in the context of social or political issues and cultural differences.

Cognitive coaching is one particularly useful strategy for peer coaching. Costa & Garmston (1985, 1986) base their cognitive coaching model on the following four assumptions:

- All behavior is determined and influenced by our perceptions.
- Teaching is decision making: before, during, and after instruction.
- Changing behavior requires an alteration or transformation of the mind.
- Human beings can continue to grow in their intellectual abilities throughout their lifetimes.

(quoted in Pajak, 1993, p. 263)

Cognitive coaching mediates, nurtures, and enhances intellectual functions, including perceptions and decision-making processes in teaching. It typically focuses on instructional practices related to student achievement, using conferencing techniques to help teachers move toward behaviors that ensure greater success for students. Cognitive coaching appeals to the rationality of teachers and works to increase their capacity to reflect on and modify instructional practices. Thus, cognitive coaching complements the more technically focused peer coaching. In peer coaching, teacher reflection is the product of the interaction between teachers. In cognitive coaching, teacher reflection is the product of the interaction between a teacher and his or her practice in the presence of another educator. The other educator could be another teacher, an administrator, or a researcher.

Costa and Garmston define the learning outcomes of cognitive coaching as a "rearrangement and restructuring of mental processes" (quoted in Pajak, 1993, p. 267). Each conference provides an opportunity for the supervisor and the teacher to learn more about themselves, each other, the students, and the subject matter being taught. Coaches strive for precise, nonjudgmental, and empathic listening while offering objective and nonjudgmental feedback. They strive to be sensitive to the teacher's preferred learning style, belief system, and level of concern. Through conferencing in this framework, participants derive greater insight into their personal belief systems. The coach's role is to expand the teacher's instructional repertoire and to create greater comfort in using a broader range of teaching strategies. Tightening up vague statements and guiding the teacher to more precise thinking is a strategy toward that goal.

Finally, Costa and Garmston view trust and learning as instrumental tools toward the building of teacher autonomy. Teachers engage in metacognitive activities that allow them to compare their values with those of others and to reexamine alternative curricular and instructional strategies. As they become more autonomous, teacher practices and thinking reflect a greater sense of efficacy (internal locus of control), flexibility (broader and alternative perspectives), precision (specificity of thought), consciousness (self-awareness), and interdependence (concern for the common good). All of these qualities help teachers better synthesize the elements of teaching they know well—the content material and the culture of schools—with elements that are less known and predictable, such as the cultural values and priorities of individual learners.

The purposes of peer coaching are to build community, common understandings, shared language, a collegial culture, and a supportive structure for teachers' acquisition of new skills. Cognitive coaching augments peer coaching by focusing on the interaction between teachers' inner thought processes and their overt instructional behaviors. Cognitive coaching encourages reflection on the meaning of this interaction. The goals of cognitive coaching (trust, learning, and autonomy) are differently oriented. Trust between the supervisor and teacher is the foundation from which teacher learning and autonomy spiral. In the cognitive coaching relationship, the supervisory function is participatory rather than presciptive, to encourage teacher autonomy. In peer coaching the primary relationship is teacher-to-teacher. Hence, the combination of peer and cognitive coaching covers a more complete range of professional practice and shifts accountability and authority to those closest to the students. Integrating the two approaches shows promise as a teacher development strategy that will lead to enriched learning environments for immigrant students.

Strategies for Developing Reflective Practice

To meet the needs of diverse learners well, teachers must be able to examine and understand how students experience their teaching. They must be able to see the classroom from the learner's perspective and to examine how their teaching decisions affect different students. This capacity for reflective practice can be encouraged in a number of ways. The recording and telling of stories about teaching experiences can facilitate reflection on the nature of professional knowledge and performance (Schon, 1983, 1987), on the meaning of social arrangements and historically embedded interactional patterns in schooling (Garman, 1986; Grant & Zeichner, 1984; Zeichner & Liston, 1987); on social justice issues within the educational context (Smyth, 1984a, 1984b, 1990; Retallick, 1990); and on the discovery of culturally responsive ways of educating immigrant and minority youth (Bowers & Flinders, 1990, 1991).

In Schon's (1983, 1987) conceptualization, teachers' stories draw on their repertoires of images and understandings about their work to help them understand everyday problems associated with it. They use past experiences as "lenses" to "frame" new situations that they encounter (Schon quoted in Pajak, 1993, p. 287). Telling stories about teaching experiences in diverse classrooms within collegial work groups can give teachers an opportunity to begin to look at the complexity of teaching and to examine, with input from others, the motives and experiences of students with backgrounds different from their own (Gomez & Tabachnik, 1992). The use of cases that raise issues of diversity and illustrate teaching decisions and practices can also prove a helpful tool for bringing to the surface and examining beliefs and assumptions along with effective teaching practices (Shulman & Mesa-Baines, 1993).

When teachers trade stories with one another and use them to examine ideas about teaching and learning, and about students and their lives, the collective repertoire of experiences is expanded. Teachers have access to more ideas and understandings about how to approach similar situations, and they may have deeper insights into their own predispositions and tendencies that allow them to name what they are doing and consider other alternatives. The larger the repertoire of stories, the greater the capacity of the teacher to resolve everyday problems.

Zeichner (see Pajak, 1993) draws on Van Manen (1977) to explain three levels of reflectivity: technical reflection, practical reflection, and critical reflection.

- **Technical reflection** focuses on the application of educational knowledge to achieve desired outcomes without considering the actual outcomes or the context in which the learning took place.
- **Practical reflection** seeks to clarify underlying assumptions, predispositions, and beliefs and the parts they play in encouraging or impeding intended educational goals.
- **Critical reflection** includes examination of issues related to justice, equity, and fulfillment in practice. Means, ends, and contexts of teaching and learning are questioned and considered against alternative approaches. The focus at this level is on broader issues and is not limited to the development of instructional skills and behaviors. It also suggests consideration of data collected through experience and research.

Zeichner and his associates (Zeichner & Hoeft, 1996; Zeichner & Liston, 1987) recommend seminars, journals, and supervisory conferences as vehicles for helping both pre- and inservice teachers attain a social reconstructionist perspective on teaching and learning. Inquiry methods suitable for this purpose include anthropological devices such as observation, action research, ethnography, and curriculum analysis. Seminars can broaden teachers' perspectives on topics including cooperative learning, multiculturalism, grouping, and assessment. Journal writing is another excellent tool for systematic self-reflection that brings to light both routine behaviors and critical incidents and uses these observations as springboards to reflective teaching. To be a reflective practitioner requires openmindedness to multiple perspectives, consideration of the consequences of one's actions from multiple perspectives, and wholeheartedness in taking control of one's own professional development. To enact these attitudes requires the technical skills of inquiry and problem solving, including observation and reasoned analysis.

The kind of observation and reasoned analysis sought can be developed through teaching events followed by grounded discussions that explore (1) the teacher's intentions, beliefs, and theoretical commitments and their relation to observed behaviors; (2) institutional and social contexts of teaching as they relate to teaching strategies; (3) analysis of instructional processes; and (4) consideration of unanticipated and hidden aspects and outcomes of the curriculum, instructional practice, and social relations in the classroom.

Several kinds of tools for reflection can be particularly useful for teachers of immigrant students in both preservice and inservice contexts. The use of autobiography can assist teachers in reflecting on their own stories and experiences. Examining one's own history, values, and beliefs can be particularly helpful to professional development in multicultural teaching (Jackson, 1992; King & Ladson-Billings, 1990; Ladson-Billings, 1995). Confronting one's ideas about teaching and one's ideals and practices can lead to greater openness to examine other possibilities. It can also help teachers to question authoritarian assumptions and practices that contribute to student dependency and docility. By discovering and reflecting on formerly unacknowledged patterns of discourse and even the role of one's family in the community, teachers can derive new insights into their relationships with others and how they interact with students. This can lead to redirection of behavior.

In addition to inquiry into the self, teachers can engage in inquiry into the lives of students, families, and communities. Some teacher education programs ask teachers to conduct child case studies to learn about how children grow, learn, think, and develop; how they experience school; and how they experience family and community. Some programs also ask teachers to conduct community case studies in which they examine the resources, customs, and mores of communities through interviews and observations of community life outside the school. Teachers learn how to become anthropologists, taking an active interest in the life of the community in which they teach.

Some other teacher education programs, like the one at Santa Clara University in California, have created immersion experiences for prospective teachers in communities that are as diverse as those in which they will later teach (King, 1991). These programs require students to live in an urban community and become involved with its institutions and in its varied settings in order to have a personal experience of the community and its people apart from the concerns of the school. This kind of experience is valuable for developing greater understanding and a broader perspective on people, their lives, and the cultural contexts of schooling. As Ladson-Billings (1995) notes,

The growing disparity between teachers' and students' backgrounds means that teachers often have little or no (or distorted) knowledge about the communities and families from which their students come. By "immersing" teacher candidates in the community they are about to serve ... the students have opportunity to observe and learn from the people they will eventually serve. Important in these immersion experiences is the opportunity to participate in planned debriefings and guided reflections lest the immersion experiences serve to reinforce students' initial prejudices. (p. 754)

Garman (1986) views reflection on these and other kinds of experiences as the heart of educational practice and as a means to generate new knowledge in the uncertain and problematic contexts of changing demographics. It can also be a means for attaining personal empowerment and building the cross-cultural sensitivity that is necessary to relate fully to immigrant children and youth. Garman differentiates between what she calls "reflection on action" and "reflection on recollection" (as reported in Pajak, 1993, p. 297). In the former, the study of immediate events in the present is the focal point; in the latter, memory of past incidents is used as data. Reflection on action involves the teacher's involvement in designing the focus of study and in anthropological data gathering. The teacher is the primary generator of knowledge. A coach may facilitate the teacher's interpretation of his or her own practice by introducing professional educational literature to help interpret the data; assisting the teacher in translating the results into a useful insight or principle; and, with the teacher, seeking other research sources to broaden their understanding.

Reflection in recollection focuses on the past to inform the present. It involves recalling images of past events; representing those images through writing or other creative representations; and interpreting the representations in terms of their meaning with reference to the present, new insights on the event, hidden meanings, emotional tone, and subliminal motives. Autobiography is one form of recollection. Examination of particular teaching or learning events in one's own life is another. Educational research and other interpretive writings are consulted to inform the interpretations and to develop more grounded assessments of what factors may actually have been at work in the situation. This is an effort to make learning from experience more purposive and more powerful by connecting it to professional knowledge and evaluating it through new perspectives.

Smyth (1984) and Retallick (1990) argue that teachers should address their practice from moral, ethical, and political perspectives and examine distortions in educational practice that are products of the established social order, such as unquestioned practices and prescribed textbooks. For example, teachers who work with immigrant students often face the problem that the hidden cultural content of the curriculum and textbooks conflicts with the beliefs and value systems of their students.

Bowers and Flinders (1991) argue that specific classroom events should be viewed as manifestations of the cultural ecology of the classroom, which can impede the academic achievement of some groups of students. They (1990) recommend that teachers become aware of issues such as the following:

- Some students from some cultures may not be familiar with linear, topic-centered narrative.
- The meanings of nonverbal behaviors like eye-contact, pauses, and body movements differ from one culture to another.
- Some cultures value cooperation and group relations over competition and individual achievement.
- Metaphors and examples that communicate clearly to students of one gender or culture may have little or no meaning for students of other genders or cultures.
- Some students rely more on subjective impressions and intuition when making decisions and forming judgments instead of relying on objective data and rational thinking.
- Traditions of some students may emphasize oral over written forms of discourse.

(quoted in Pajak, 1993, p. 303)

Professional development that addresses these issues can help teachers of immigrant students (1) recognize taken-for-granted language and cultural patterns that may affect student learning, (2) clarify their judgments, and (3) adapt practices to take into account student differences. The culturally responsive professional developer or coach also takes into account the choices that he or she makes when providing feedback to teachers. As connoisseurs of the role of language and culture, in learning, facilitators should focus teachers' attention on concerns related to issues such as race, gender, language, and national origin and help them understand that objectivity may be illusory when we are shaped by differing cultural experiences and contexts.

Enacting Collaboration

In addition to these specific strategies for engaging teachers in productive learning, school organizational structures must be redesigned so that they actively support staff learning and collaboration around serious problems of practice. This requires rethinking schedules, staffing patterns, and grouping arrangements to create blocks of time for teachers to work and learn together. In addition, schools must be organized around small, cohesive units that structure ongoing collaborative work among groups of adults and students (e.g., teaching teams or clusters, houses, or advisories) so that teachers have shared knowledge of students and shared responsibilities for designing their work with students. This has been done in restructured schools in a variety of ways, ranging from block scheduling, to reallocations of staff so that all have direct responsibilities for students, to creating more time for shared teacher work (Darling-Hammond, Ancess, & Falk, 1995; Darling-Hammond et al., 1993; Short,1991).

Contemporary research and theoretical literature support the notion that interdisciplinary team teaching, which relies on distributed expertise, can provide teachers with a peer support structure that facilitates the adoption or alteration of pedagogical approaches. This section explores the implications of teaming in combination with more integrative curriculum as professional development tools to assist teachers in viewing the teaching of language as an integral part of instruction across disciplines. Teaming can be particularly beneficial to teachers working with immigrant students, because it allows teachers to share with each other what they know about teaching strategies and about individual learners. We also encourage the use of constructivist approaches as tools to empower teachers by helping them become effective learners as well as teachers.

Team Teaching

Interdisciplinary team teaching supplies a context that can create community and mobilize collegiality among educators. According to Alexander and George (1981), it can afford teachers

the opportunity for improved instruction due to the teachers' combined knowledge of student needs, increased integration of content areas, continued evaluation of the curriculum and of student progress, improved intellectual stimulation, enhanced communication between teachers and parents and a personalized climate for learning. (quoted in Pink & Hyde, 1992, pp. 117-118)

Integrative curriculum seeks linkages and relationships among disciplines rather than emphasizing the boundaries between them. It also encourages multiple perspectives on themes and life experiences. Hence, integrated curriculum and multicultural education are compatible partners in educating culturally diverse learners.

The exercise of team teaching is professional development in action. It involves much more than a group of teachers working with the same group of students. By working together, teachers share knowledge. For a team to be successful, however, the work must be meaningful, and it must engender shared responsibility and accountability. There should be a set of core values that guide behavior and opportunities to provide feedback to one another about plans, ideas, and performance. The group should be of heterogeneous composition in terms of areas of expertise. Not all the members of a team need to be expert in teaching English. It is extremely important, however, that at least one member of a team have experience and expertise in the use of strategies for working with students who are learning English. The combination of these conditions can create a pedagogy that empowers immigrant students to participate more effectively in school, because they are surrounded by teacher expertise in a variety of areas.

Though there are problems associated with team teaming (e.g., logistics related to times and places for team meetings as well as personality conflicts among team members that inhibit team building), the promise for teachers is great. Interdisciplinary teaming decreases the isolation felt by many teachers, especially those who have not had much experience with immigrant students or who have worked only in more traditional settings. It encourages open communication and dialogue about students and strategies among teachers. Teachers benefit from the insights of colleagues and have the opportunity to share responsibilities with others. The opportunity for participatory problem solving and decision making is the greatest strength of collaborative teaching, because it gives teachers increased authority and accountability over day-to-day classroom operations. Linking teachers and classrooms within a team creates a "collective autonomy" (Darling-Hammond, 1986) that increases shared knowledge and norms of practice. Teaming also creates a new organizational unit in the school that better equips teachers to meet all students, including the immigrant student.

School–Home Collaboratives

Another excellent, but often neglected, set of resources for professional development are the families, communities, and organizations with a vested interest in the welfare of immigrant students. When teachers, using anthropological research methodologies, go into the community to gather information about families and community resources, they acquire authentic information firsthand and develop an understanding of the interaction patterns in the homes and communities in which their students live. Giving students opportunities to share their experiences and views in class is also useful for building teachers' knowledge about them.

When teachers conduct research in the communities they serve, they give themselves the advantage of interacting with the social networks that provide supports for students and their families. The essential feature of social networks is the exchange of "funds of knowledge, the cultural practices and bodies of knowledge and information that cultural groups use to survive, to get ahead, or to thrive" (Moll, 1992, p.

21). These funds of knowledge represent a major social and intellectual resource for schools.

Professional development that taps into the community's funds of knowledge can take a variety of forms. It can mean having teachers conduct household visits to meet parents; hold parent–teacher conferences; and document families' social histories, origins, work histories, and other historically accumulated and culturally developed bodies of knowledge and skills. After-school settings, such as community-based youth programs and parent centers, serve as social contexts for informing, assisting, and supporting teachers' work. Such settings provide teachers and researchers a social context to learn about the community. Tapping into the community's funds of knowledge benefits everyone. Students and other community members can make connections with the schools and provide culturally authentic material that enriches teachers' and students' intellectual capacities as well as their attitudes and beliefs about each other.

As we have seen, new professional development models, structures, and practices are not static and unchanging; neither are they straightforward and formulaic. They are certainly vastly different from the traditional model of delivering knowledge to teachers by talking to them. Shared leadership among teachers, administrators, and community members can create a climate of trust that can lead to greater risk taking and consequent growth among all participants in the educational enterprise. But such a climate is difficult to develop even in relatively homogeneous school communities. It is even more difficult to stimulate in culturally diverse settings where role expectations may differ among school and community leaders. Participants should be prepared to encounter moments of dissonance as they struggle to understand and practice these new ways of becoming more effective. Strategies that value community, collegiality, and collaboration require long-range organizational work as well as pedagogical investments. In the next chapter, we examine several examples of professional development strategies for pre- and inservice teachers that illustrate the qualities we have outlined in this chapter.

Programs That Prepare Teachers to Work Effectively With Immigrant Students

As the need for teachers to learn to teach immigrant students has grown more obvious, schools and teacher education programs have begun to respond by rethinking their strategies for supporting the professional development of bilingual and monolingual teachers. This chapter describes five programs that reflect different approaches to the preparation of teachers for working with immigrant youth: Three are preservice teacher education programs, and two represent approaches to inservice teacher development. These approaches illustrate the principles discussed in earlier chapters. The descriptions focus on the programs' goals, frames of reference, and key features.

Some of these programs are supported by changes in educational policy at the state, district, or university level. Perhaps most far-reaching is California's decision to adopt new expectations and standards for monolingual teachers that explicitly address their ability to meet the needs of bilingual and immigrant students. California's Cross-Cultural Language and Academic Development (CLAD) Credential is based on the recognition that teaching students from a variety of linguistic and cultural backgrounds whose primary language is not English is part of most teachers' jobs, not just the terrain of "special" teachers. The goal of the program is to equip teaching candidates with skills and knowledge in three areas: language acquisition and development, culture, and pedagogical strategies for teaching new English language learners in the content areas. Below we describe programs for preparing teachers for the CLAD certificate at San Diego State University and the University of California, Santa Barbara, as well as a program at the University of Minnesota that prepares teachers to work with both English and non-English speakers from a comprehensive perspective.

We then describe the approaches to ongoing professional development in use at The International High School in New York City, one of the nation's most successful schools engaged in educating immigrant youth. Finally, we report on the building of learning communities in the Bilingual Cooperative Integrated Reading and Composition (BCIRC) Model developed at Johns Hopkins University and used in a number of schools and districts in the United States.

In these and other emerging programs, immigrants and new English language learners are not viewed from a deficit perspective as needing pull-out courses for remediation, but rather as learners whose access to challenging content can be enhanced through teaching strategies that provide multiple pathways to the understanding of language and content together. This perspective transforms the teacher's role to one of an access provider rather than a gatekeeper. Kuhlman and Vidal (1993) argue that teachers should be educated in ways that enable them to challenge the role of schools in maintaining the status quo of social class, race, and gender inequities. "Teachers need to act as facilitators, collaborating and reciprocating with students in order to empower them, rather than controlling and mystifying them" (p. 100).

This philosophy views second language teaching from a macro perspective that incorporates the social, cultural, and political contexts of language, rather than a micro perspective that looks at second language teaching as a set of discrete teaching behaviors. Clair's (1993) observations about ESL and bilingual teachers are equally applicable to other teachers as well:

The nature of ... teachers' job responsibilities makes the inclusion of the larger context all the more important in preservice second language teacher preparation programs. Regardless of where one is aligned in the debate about the purposes of ESL and bilingual education and the nature of L2 (second language) development, there is at least one indisputable goal. That is, teaching language ... is a minimal responsibility. ... ESL/bilingual teachers must not only teach language, but they must teach students how to use [language] as a vehicle to acquire academic content. Therefore, it is essential that ESL/bilingual teachers understand the greater context within which their language-minority students fit, which includes at minimum, understanding the demands of the mainstream classroom, the mainstream teachers' challenges and concerns, the culture of the school and the community. (p. 242)

Programs that operate from an integrative perspective on language and learning prepare teachers to see their students and their students' learning holistically. They seek to offset the problems that Tedick and Walker

(1994, 1995) identify as having traditionally plagued second language teacher education, as follows:

• **Failure to see the interconnectedness between first and second languages and cultures.** This disjointedness has serious impact on the structure and pedagogy of second language education and has especially negative consequences for language minority students.

In second language instruction, there are different expectations for majority and minority students. While schools encourage native English speakers to begin second language study during adolescence, they compel students with a potential for bilingualism (who bring other languages skills to the school setting) to work rapidly and often unrealistically to acquire fluent English language and literacy skills and give no attention to their continued first language development. (1994, p. 302)

This approach minimizes the interconnections between first and second language development and reduces the potential for advancement in both languages. For language minority students, the inattention to first language development is detrimental to academic achievement. Teacher preparation programs should enable future teachers to view second language development from a perspective that includes first language development, while recognizing the uniqueness of specific languages and cultures.

• **Fragmentation and isolation of language teaching and learning.** In both colleges and schools, bilingual education, foreign language, and language arts programs are often the responsibility of distinctly separate administrative entities. This kind of isolation makes it difficult for staff members as well as students to communicate across programs and to benefit from increased communication across the fields.

Second language learning for language minority students remains remedial and compensatory in its conceptualization and delivery (indeed it is not uncommon to find ESL paired with special education for administrative purposes in the public schools), and very little cross dialogue occurs between professionals serving these students and their majority language counterparts. Sadly, successes and failures in one field do not often serve as learning opportunities for other language education fields. (1995, p. 501)

• **The pervasive view of language as object.** This view leads to a narrow focus on components of language phonology, morphology, syntax, and lexicon. Such a narrow focus on the pieces of a language denies the social nature of language as a tool for communication and a mechanism through which content can be explored and examined. Language study is generally decontextualized and unrelated to the lives of students, their school, or the community, and much of language instruction remains grammar driven and primarily teacher directed.

• **A paralyzing focus on methodology.** Historically, preparation programs for foreign language and ESL teachers have focused intensely on instructional methods rather than the what, why, and who of second language instruction. Tedick and Walker argue that this focus on methodology has made second language instruction teacher centered, by focusing on the ways in which the teacher best organizes, presents, and assesses lessons. Such a narrow focus has insulated second language teachers from the growing knowledge about language—evident in the fields of adult education, literacy development, and early childhood education—that supports a view of language development as "an integrated, generative process in which the learner is an active agent" (1994, p. 306). The focus on methodology, though useful, can also ignore the important reality of social, political, and economic contexts and their impact on teaching and learning.

• **A disjuncture between language and culture.** In many teacher education programs, culture is accorded a minimal role.

In general, culture is treated in the majority of both ESL and foreign language settings as an interesting application, or a pleasant add-on, always secondary to the more important linguistic content. In ESL instruction, culture takes a back seat not only to language, but also to content area study. (1994, p. 308)

Sometimes the study of culture has a distinctly assimilationist emphasis. Often it is superficial and promotes stereotypes. Tedick and Walker
argue that

Prospective second language teachers need to have a clear understanding of themselves
as cultural beings, of the variety of worldviews espoused by participants in the target culture and the native culture, and of the need to view both cultures from a number of different perspectives. Such understandings will not be achieved by simply adding more culture
courses to the curriculum that prospective teachers follow. Instead, just as culture must be
an integral part of second language pedagogy, so too must it become an integral part of
teacher education programs, including attention to school culture and classroom ecology.
(1994, p. 309)

Preservice Teacher Education Programs

The Second Languages and Cultures Education Program—University of Minnesota

The Second Languages and Cultures Education program (SLC) at the
University of Minnesota is designed with the core problems outlined
above in mind. The program is based on the notion that "second language teachers' practice needs to combat these ingrained problems"
(Tedick & Walker, 1995, p. 503), and students in the SLC program are
continuously challenged to examine and to find solutions. This
postbaccalaureate program combines the preparation of foreign language and English as a second language teachers. The combination
seeks to lessen the degree of isolation experienced by language teachers and the degree of fragmentation in the field of language learning.

Course of study
Students typically complete the program over a period of 15 months.
The students who enter the program tend to be older than average,
with a mean age of 29. Candidates are selected on the basis of academic
background, advanced language proficiency, previous exposure to
cross-cultural settings, and experience working in educational settings.

The program is based on the philosophical tenets that "teachers and students both act as knowers and learners in an active, experiential, and integrative process; that teaching is context sensitive; and that reflection is a cornerstone in teacher development" (Tedick & Walker, 1995, p. 503). Field experiences and university-based studies take place concurrently. "We believe that it is imperative for our students to have ongoing school experiences that provide a context for our discussions about pedagogy and the culture of schooling" (Tedick & Walker, 1994, p. 508). Students register each quarter for three courses: Curriculum, Instruction, and Clinical Experience. In these courses, they explore issues and questions that reflect the 10 themes that form the core of the program, described below. Additionally, students register for a research component during their first year of teaching.

In the state of Minnesota, ESL certification is for grades K-12. Thus candidates are required to have classroom experience at both the elementary and secondary school levels. Students are placed in different settings: "pull-out," "push-in" or "collaborative inclusion" programs, and self-contained classrooms. Throughout the year, they are exposed to experiences in urban and suburban settings and in traditional and alternative programs. "Experiences in such a wide variety of contexts help students to develop a sense of the big picture, of the interrelatedness of second language education contexts" (Tedick & Walker, 1995, p. 509).

Ten themes form the core of the program and define its content as well as its processes: language and culture; the language learner; integration of curriculum, instruction, and learner characteristics; theory and research bases for second language teaching and learning; school culture and second languages; development of self as a teacher; assessment; diversity as a natural human experience; growth in perspective through research; and intensive classroom experience at both the elementary and secondary levels. The work that students do in relation to these themes is described below.

Language and culture—the human element: Students study the meanings of language and culture learning, the ways that self-expression relates to language learning contexts, the relationship between language and culture, the relation of language and cultural identity to self-concept, and the role of teachers in promoting language development and cultural understanding in students as well as other adults.

The language learner: Students explore the unique characteristics of second language learners and how these may affect their interest and participation in second language teaching settings.

Integration of curriculum, instruction, and learner characteristics: Students consider the impact of curriculum perspectives on teaching, including wrestling with issues of how societal and school-based perspectives on curriculum and instruction influence practice and how positive learning experiences can be created that attend to student needs within the constraints of the school context.

Theory and research bases for second language teaching and learning: Students consider the theoretical and research foundations of teaching and the ways in which teachers can view and use their own research and that of others to create positive learning experiences.

School culture and second languages: Students explore the social context of schooling and its impact on teachers and learners.

Development of self as a teacher: Students consider the roles of teachers and the process of teacher development from a personal perspective.

Assessment: Students examine ways of assessing student language learning and the ways in which testing and assessment affect curriculum and teaching.

Diversity as a natural human experience: Students explore ways in which teachers can help students appreciate the human experience as multicultural and multilingual and consider the implications of human diversity for teaching.

Growth in perspective through research: This theme explores questions such as, "In what ways can my own observations inform me about the processes of teaching and learning? How can I become a teacher researcher? How can I continue to grow as a teacher through systematic exploration of myself, my teaching, and my students?"

Intensive classroom experience at both the elementary and secondary levels: Students reflect on their experience and its impact on their development, asking, for example, "How does time and experience with diverse age groups—and extended work with experienced teachers—contribute to my growth as a teacher?"

Students in the SLC program are organized into cohort groups, referred to as "a community of developing teachers," where they work together and have shared experiences in their development. These cohort groups are further divided into "base groups" and "feedback session groups." A graduate assistant usually facilitates the base group and keeps close contact with teaching candidates through conferences, journals, and on-site visits and observations. Through base groups, students are able to share their experiences with one another and get feedback on their work. In the feedback sessions, developing teachers view microteaching videos (focused videos on one element of their own or others' classroom practice) as well as more globally oriented videos of their actual teaching in the schools. In addition to base groups and feedback sessions, students participate in "work days"—days set aside to work on group projects. Graduates continue to be members of cohort groups for their first year of teaching in order to participate in monthly seminars at the university and to engage in action research projects leading to their Master's degrees in education.

Student assessment

Assessment of growth and development of teaching candidates relies on reflection and self-evaluation as well as feedback from peers, cooperating teachers, and staff. Assessment of students is centered around several issues: personal development, understanding of learners, curriculum development, instruction, and research.

Focus on personal development: Students are asked to maintain a portfolio that includes several pieces of their writing related to their experiences, assignments they have done in the term, teaching units, materials, lessons, samples of student work, records of student feedback, and written evaluations of their teaching.

Focus on the learner: Students conduct a case study of a second language learner. This usually involves gathering as much information as possible about the learner through his or her work, interviews, and observations in a variety of educational and social situations.

Focus on curriculum development: During the course of the year, students are asked to develop at least three curriculum units. They are required to work on at least one of the units individually and the other(s) collectively.

Focus on instruction: At the beginning of the fall and winter quarters, students engage in microteaching practice every week. They submit a copy of lesson plans to colleagues and peers for feedback and videotape and critique one of their lessons.

Focus on research: During the first year, students choose a topic that they wish to investigate. Research methodology and skills are addressed in monthly seminars throughout the course of the year. This helps to prepare teachers for critical analysis and the ability to make change.

These features of the program illustrate the connections between a restructured vision of teachers' roles and language learning, culture, and content. The next horizon is to create closer connections with schools and between pre-and inservice teacher learning opportunities.

As teacher education programs *themselves* engage in a process of self-reflection and re-form and seek to establish stronger links with the changing world of schools, how can they develop mutually beneficial relationships with those schools in a way that encourages a cycle of renewal both for inservice as well as preservice teachers? How can we change both the preparation of teachers and the classroom settings in which we prepare them to teach? As continually developing teachers ourselves, we need to examine what we do, how it affects our students, and what might be options for the future. (Tedick & Walker, 1995, p. 513)

These questions face all programs that are seeking to prepare teachers for new learners. Similar themes arise in the California-based programs we describe below.

The Cross-Cultural Language and Academic Development Program (CLAD)—San Diego State University

The preservice teacher education program at San Diego State University seeks to prepare teachers to work with English language learners where bilingual programs are not available or to work in the English component of a bilingual program using specially designed English language development strategies. These pedagogical strategies include Specially Designed Academic Instruction in English, sometimes called sheltered instruction, which involves instruction in a subject area, delivered in English by a content-area-certified teacher, that is specially designed to provide English learners access to the curriculum. This is increasingly important at the secondary school level, where students may otherwise be denied access to core academic instruction when bilingual teachers are not available.

Program design
Preservice candidates can move from the monolingual (CLAD) program to the bilingual (B/CLAD) program as they become proficient in

a second language, or they can later take additional preparation to become B/CLAD specialists (Kuhlman & Vidal, 1993). The CLAD emphasis is offered within specified blocks of existing credential programs and requires completion of both additional course work and field experience supervised by master teachers and university faculty. Before being admitted to the program, CLAD candidates are expected to verify experience in learning a second language. This requirement can be met through nine quarter hours of college course work in a second language or a prolonged period of residence in a country where the language spoken was not the native language (e.g., Peace Corps training). A large number of students fulfill this requirement through six semester units of course work. The CLAD program also requires that candidates "demonstrate the knowledge, values, and skills for operationalizing a culturally pluralistic school curriculum that specifically addresses the linguistic, cultural, and racial backgrounds of our ethnically diverse school communities" (Kuhlman & Vidal, 1993, pp. 108-109).

Prospective teachers also have to meet prerequisite course requirements to enter the program. To fulfill the prerequisite for the Language Acquisition/Development component, candidates take the following courses: Linguistics and English, Child Language Acquisition, and Theory and Practice of English as a Second Language. Candidates are expected to complete Introduction to Multicultural Education and Bilingual Teaching Strategies to fulfill the prerequisites for the Cross-Cultural/Multicultural Education and Pedagogy components, respectively. Principles and practices of English language development and cross-cultural/multicultural education are infused into the core methods courses. Assignments in these courses have included an alternative algorithm assignment in which students were asked to interview members of another culture on how they learned a particular math function, developing a multicultural literature unit, developing a global unit, shadowing a language minority student, and simulations to experience the effects of prejudice and cultural differences.

Content methods courses in mathematics, social studies, science, reading, and language arts include attention to culture and pedagogical methods for new English language learners. Other requirements include psychological foundations of education—with an emphasis on culture, language, and language acquisition—and student teaching experiences and seminars. Students are placed for at least one semester with a Master Teacher who has obtained a Language Development Specialist certificate or credential and has a significant number of new English learners.

The CLAD program aims to develop knowledge and skills in the following competency areas identified by the California Commission on Teacher Credentialing: cultural awareness; theoretical knowledge of linguistics and language acquisition, as applied to ESL and bilingual education; content knowledge; knowledge of pedagogical methods for second language learners; and fieldwork (Kuhlman & Vidal, 1993).

Cultural awareness: During their preparation program, students may study multicultural education or sociolinguistics at the undergraduate level as well as humanistic, social, behavioral, and psychological aspects of teaching. "The core curriculum should address issues of cultural diversity, cultural conflict, cultural pluralism, cultural assimilation, and relationships between cultural diversity, educational equity, academic achievement, and socioeconomic status" (Kuhlman & Vidal, 1993, p. 104).

Theoretical knowledge: Students are expected to become knowledgeable about language phonology, morphology, and syntax; first and second language acquisition; the structure and role of language in terms of linguistic components and social function; analytic aspects of the English language for purposes of teaching limited English proficient students; philosophy and theory of bilingual and bicultural education; techniques and materials in ESL teaching; and the effects of attitudes and motivation on language learning and acquisition.

Content knowledge: Students are expected to complete an undergraduate academic major before being admitted to the preservice program. This requirement is important because "applying specially designed English language development strategies to content makes learning English more meaningful and has direct application to the mainstream classroom. It serves to empower students both in English language skills and content areas simultaneously" (Kuhlman & Vidal, 1993, p. 105).

Knowledge of pedagogical methods: These include total physical response, natural approach, content-based instruction, cooperative learning, and whole language teaching strategies. Both courses and fieldwork are organized to ensure opportunities to acquire these methods.

Fieldwork: This includes practice teaching, classroom observations, and community ethnographies.

Program implementation and impact

In preparation for the implementation of the CLAD credential in 1992, nine university faculty members representing different areas of study (language arts, mathematics, educational psychology, science, and social studies) participated in a year-long pilot program to build their own capacity to prepare prospective teachers and to begin to integrate the program ideas into their courses. The main charge of the faculty was to develop strategies to infuse relevant content in their teacher preparation courses. The topics were chosen after a needs assessment of the faculty. They included the following: understanding cultural diversity; understanding language structure, language learning, and language acquisition; developing expertise across the disciplines and in various cultural settings with effective teaching strategies for English language development; expanding knowledge of community resources and the home environment; and enhancing knowledge about bilingual models such as maintenance, two-way bilingual, immersion, and transitional bilingual education (Ross, 1994, p. 430).

The faculty development program began with a one-week course designed to build increased knowledge in the areas of language and culture, bilingual models, and ways to infuse related concepts and pedagogical strategies into methods courses. In addition, there were opportunities throughout the year for faculty to discuss, integrate, and make changes to their courses throughout the year. There were five additional all-day workshops, and faculty met twice a month to discuss issues related to the program. They also had access to an outside consultant to provide assistance in planning instructional activities and locating resources.

Researchers at San Diego State University designed a study to assess the results of faculty training and its impact on student teacher preparation. The study analyzed faculty syllabi before and after training to see whether core concepts were present or absent. It also analyzed data from six hours of structured faculty discussions and surveyed both a pilot group and a comparison group of students.

The pilot group included 25 monolingual English-speaking teacher candidates who took part in the program during its first year. Content in language acquisition and cultural pedagogy was infused into their course work in educational psychology, social studies, language arts, science, and math. For their student teaching, students were placed in professional development schools with Master Teachers who held Language Development Specialist credentials and attended seminars. A group of student teachers who had completed a traditional credential program served as the comparison group for purposes of the study.

Students completed a 20-item questionnaire asking their opinion of the effectiveness of the CLAD program on various dimensions of preparation for teaching diverse students and new English language learners, followed by a 30-minute interview regarding strengths and weaknesses of the program. They were also asked to imagine a class of students with at least five different language backgrounds and to describe the steps they would take to ensure equal access to the curriculum for all of the students. As a comparison, 10 randomly selected student teachers in the traditional credential program were asked to respond to the same scenario (Ross, 1994).

Results of the study were very positive. Ross (1994) notes, "it appears that the year-long process took faculty from the additive stage of multicultural infusion to the threshold of transformation" (p. 437). Analysis of faculty discourse revealed a progression from concerns about the meaning and definition of CLAD to a focus on a wide array of cross-curricular goals to be pursued in the future. These included increasing sensitivity to cultural differences, broadening of the educational environment, understanding global linkages, and promoting higher order thinking skills and collaborative learning.

Students in the CLAD group perceived themselves to be considerably better prepared to meet the needs of diverse learners than students in the traditional program. Compared to their counterparts, students in the CLAD program rated their program as being effective in dealing with the nature of culture (72% vs. 46%); helping them establish a positive affective environment in multicultural classrooms (86% vs. 46%); understanding the dynamics of prejudice (67% vs. 46%); all areas of language structure and acquisition (71% vs. 27%); most areas of pedagogy, especially building on prior knowledge (81% vs. 50%); the use of first language literacy in second language instruction (62% vs. 36%); English language development strategies (86% vs. 41%); bilingual methods and strategies (62% vs. 32%); content-based sheltered instruction (62% vs. 0%); and developing curriculum sensitive to cognitive and contextual dimensions of instruction (72% vs. 50%).

While CLAD students asked for more integration into methods courses of pedagogical strategies for multicultural, linguistically diverse classrooms, they also noted a number of strengths of the pilot program, including its prerequisites; the cultural information it provided; its teaching strategies, methods, and approaches; and student teaching. In their responses to the scenario question, CLAD students were more likely to focus on curricular approaches and cultural infusion strategies to meeting students' needs, while comparison group students were more likely to talk about assessing students for special education services or adding discrete cultural elements to the curriculum (Banks's [1984] lowest level of multicultural infusion). The researchers concluded that the CLAD program seems to have successfully promoted a model of education in which diverse cultural and linguistic backgrounds are viewed as assets and resources for instruction. The tendency of the comparison group to focus on academic and subject matter assessments of students as opposed to language proficiency and cultural data might be construed as reflecting a deficit perspective (Ross, 1994, p. 433).

The university's efforts to design new teacher preparation strategies appear to be making a difference in how new teachers approach their classrooms and their students, which should provide a strong foundation on which they can build their career-long practice. To illustrate how similar ideas have taken a somewhat different shape, we also review the CLAD program at the University of California, Santa Barbara.

The Cross-Cultural Language and Academic Development Program (CLAD)—University of California, Santa Barbara

The Teacher Education Program at the University of California, Santa Barbara offers the Multiple Subject Teaching Credential with a (Bilingual) Cross-Cultural Language and Academic Development Emphasis in Spanish (BCLAD/CLAD). All students, regardless of the certification they are pursuing, receive instruction in English Language Development and Specially Designed Academic Instruction in English, which is integrated throughout the Multiple Subject Program. Although this program is focused on the training of elementary and middle school teachers, we describe it here because many of its strategies could be usefully applied to the preparation of high school teachers as well.

The 5-year program is two tiered, consisting of a first tier of undergraduate study in the Multiple Subject Matter program and a second tier, a fifth year of teacher preparation. This discussion focuses on the fifth year.

The program is organized around six themes that are reflected in both course work and student teaching: philosophy of education, study of children and schools, methodological competence, collegiality, reflection, and diversity.

Philosophy of education: Through interactive journaling, students derive a deeper understanding of their own culture and its power in shaping their understanding of other cultures. Students write journal entries throughout their preservice teacher education experience. Periodically, along with university faculty, they reflect on these entries to elicit their underlying meaning and to identify patterns in their own thinking about cultural diversity. Once students bring these patterns to light, they can scrutinize more critically their own behaviors and their underlying cultural foundations. With this knowledge, they can then sharpen the focus of their philosophies of education and multicultural education, so that they align more closely and are more compatible with the characteristics of a language-diverse student population.

Study of children and schools: The program holds the view that to understand student learning, teachers must be able to observe children closely and learn from these observations. Since learning takes place in a complex context where many factors converge, teachers must study the whole environment and how it influences a child's school experience in order to understand the way the child makes sense of subject matter. Prospective teachers take courses in psychological and social foundations of schooling that include conducting ethnographic case studies. The first is a case study of a child in the classroom in which the teacher candidate is student teaching; the second is a case study of this classroom and the school. In both cases, candidates are expected to become familiar with the families and the communities of the students with whom they work.

Methodological competence is developed using the California state curriculum frameworks as a centerpiece. Work focuses on the need to provide quality education for an increasingly diverse student body and on how to adapt curriculum and teaching to meet the needs of all students. The close relationship between coursework and fieldwork provides candidates an opportunity to integrate theory and practice.

Collegiality: Students are trained in collegial coaching, which means they receive instruction in communication skills, data gathering tools, and feedback skills. As part of their student teaching experience, they participate in repetitive cycles of collegial coaching in which they visit one anothers' classrooms and observe each other teach. In January, they engage in what is called a "linguistic switch": Those in the regular teacher education program spend two days in a bilingual classroom, and vice-versa; they then share their experiences in a seminar.

Reflection is a cornerstone of the program. Most of the writing assignments and almost every course have components requiring student reflection. Students keep reflective journals through which they engage in dialogue with supervisors and faculty, and they develop two portfolios over the course of the 11-month program. Supervisory groups are composed of student teachers who work at the same school for the entire year and meet with university supervisors weekly. Issues and concerns are explored as they arise from the experiences of the student teachers in the group. The groups are designed for professional support, and most usually become a closely knit community.

Diversity is addressed in a number of ways. Students in the Multiple Subject Teaching Credential program are encouraged to enroll in the bilingual course sequence, and most other courses address diversity issues explicitly. For their clinical experience, students spend two semesters in schools. At least one of the schools has to have ethnically, socially, and economically diverse student populations. All but one of the six supervisory groups includes bilingual student teachers. This ensures that bilingual and multicultural issues are likely to become part of the agenda for all student teachers participating in those groups.

Students at each of the three cooperating schools are organized in small cohort groups, which gives them the opportunity to reflect on their experience and provide support to each other. All three schools have bilingual programs. While the particular models used in these schools vary, the sheltered content instruction model is typical. The program recognizes that not all placements are consistent with the program's philosophy and tries to prepare students for that.

Most of the students in the program, even those who are not in the Bilingual Education strand, elect to complete the three-course bilingual education sequence, which is open to all students. This includes Teaching Strategies for Bilingual Cross-Cultural Education, Bilingual Language Arts Curriculum, and Bilingual Methods and Procedures.

The **Teaching Strategies for Bilingual Cross-Cultural Education** course explores the following issues: theoretical framework of bilingual education, language learning in bilingual settings, assessment and diagnosis of language proficiency, research and its impact on policy for bilingual education in California, and immigration issues.

In the **Bilingual Language Arts Curriculum,** taught in Spanish, students explore the theory, rationale, and practical applications associated with a complete Spanish Language Arts program in bilingual classrooms. Reading and writing approaches to the teaching of language arts in bilingual settings are introduced.

Bilingual Methods and Procedures explores the various models of bilingual education and the contexts that shape them. The course also focuses on why primary language instruction is important for development of other language competencies; the various transition programs from primary language instruction to English that are supportive of second-language and first-language development; and the pros and cons of bilingual education, intended to prepare teachers to clearly articulate their work and why it is important.

All of the students in the postbaccalaureate program (not just those in the Bilingual Education program) are required to take a course in **Understanding Social and Linguistic Factors in Teaching English as a Second Language.** Issues explored in this course include understanding second language acquisition, teaching methods, and strategies; assessing student learning; curriculum and materials development; strategies for sheltered language instruction; and the why, where, and how of bilingual education. Assignments are designed to uncover the theoretical underpinnings of practice.

The program takes the position that multicultural education issues need to be infused into every aspect of teaching and learning and encourages students to approach their work with this perspective. In the past few years, the program has moved to infuse social, cultural, and linguistic issues into all the courses offered in the Multiple Subject Credential program. This has led to the integration of the ideas described above into a single team-taught course.

Recently, in an effort to support faculty and staff in implementing these new concepts in their work, the program launched an inservice training program for instructors and supervisors. They meet once a month to explore issues related to the CLAD, especially how to infuse these concepts into courses, seminars, and supervision.

Inservice Teacher Development

The International High School—New York City

The International High School was founded in 1985 as a collaborative project of the New York City Board of Education and the Board of Higher Education. The school serves recent immigrants and thus accepts only students who have been in the United States for a period of 4 years or less and who score in the bottom 21% of the English Language Battery Exam. In keeping with one of the thrusts of the school restructuring movement, the school is small in size—approximately

460 students from over 50 countries speaking over 35 languages—which has allowed it to develop a distinctive culture and sense of community (Bryk & Driscoll, 1988; Sizer, 1984). In the decade since its founding, International has developed a coherent set of innovations consisting of educational principles, pedagogical practices, curricular materials, governance arrangements, and professional development institutions. On the basis of these innovations, the school has attracted attention for a string of achievements in educating the primarily low-income minority students who make up its population. It has won numerous awards. It boasts of an attendance rate of over 90%, a graduation rate of 90–95%, a college-going rate of over 90%, and a pass rate on New York State Competency Tests of virtually 100% annually.

Perhaps the best starting point for understanding International's educational framework is found in the educational principles that underlie the school's approach to instruction:

1. Limited English proficient students require the ability to understand, speak, read, and write English with near-native fluency to realize their full potential in an English-speaking society.
2. Fluency in a language other than English must be viewed as a resource for the student, the school, and the society.
3. Language skills are most effectively learned in context and when embedded in a content area.
4. The most successful educational programs are those that emphasize rigorous standards coupled with effective support systems.
5. Attempts to group students homogeneously in an effort to make instruction more manageable preclude the way in which adolescents learn best, i.e., from each other.
6. The carefully planned use of multiple learning contexts in addition to the classroom (e.g., learning centers, career internship sites, field trips) facilitates language acquisition and content-area mastery.
7. Career education is a significant motivational factor for adolescent learners.
8. The most effective instruction takes place when teachers actively participate in the school decision-making process, including instructional program design, curriculum development, materials selection, faculty hiring, staff training, and peer evaluation.

(International High School: *Educational Philosophy*)

These principles embody four fundamental conceptual building blocks of International's philosophy: (1) a linguistic methodology that assumes that language skills are best learned through the use of content material and in context; (2) a commitment to both English and native language development; (3) heterogeneous small-group student collaboration on experiential, activity-based projects; and (4) small-group faculty collaboration on both instructional planning and school-wide governance. These approaches have been developed hand-in-hand since the first year of the school's operation. In many ways, the process was driven by the last building block: the institutionalized pattern of collaboration among teachers and administrators.

Small-group faculty collaboration

International's principal chose the seven experienced teachers who made up the teaching staff in the first year of the school's operation. He then turned over responsibility to this group for hiring the additional teachers for the second year, an approach he dubbed "student empowerment through teacher professionalism." The seven teachers formed a hiring committee and selected their colleagues. A curriculum committee was added in the second year, followed by a staff development committee in the third year in order to assure that the teachers were being supported in their responsibilities. Eventually, a "school support team" was formed from representatives of all the committees to coordinate policy decisions of the school. In all these groups, decisions are made by consensus.

The committees played two important roles in the evolution of the school's educational practices: First, they provided forums in which faculty ideas could be discussed, refined, and implemented in a planned fashion. Second, participation on committees exposed each faculty member to the experience of working in teams, which they usually found to be productive. This experience led the faculty to experiment in ever more extensive ways with cooperative work groups for student learning as well.

The faculty's willingness to take collective responsibility for their own professional development began slowly during the first few years. A "student-for-a-day" program is an example of the kind of small steps that were used to break down the traditional resistance of teachers to opening up their classrooms to other adults. Teachers were freed of their responsibilities for a day, provided they spent the entire day following a student from class to class. After a few months, most of the faculty had taken advantage of the opportunity, and the discussions that followed led to a revision of the school schedule to allow for longer class periods (70 minutes), so that teachers would have larger instructional blocks in which to teach and plan their activities. The "student-for-a-day" program led many teachers to continue visiting each others' classes, which in turn spawned the formation of peer support groups, in which teachers would regularly meet to discuss their observations of each others' teaching as well as instructional ideas in general.

By the fifth year of the school's existence, professional development had become institutionalized at International. The staff development committee planned school-wide colloquia and seminars, while the personnel committee oversaw a process of peer review in which each teacher convenes a peer support group that works with him or her on a review process that includes observations, conversation, and assembling a portfolio of teaching work. Teachers write their own self-evaluations periodically, which are added to peer and administrative assessments. These developments also had implications for students, as both portfolios and self–peer–administrator assessments were later adapted for use with student work groups (as self–peer–teacher assessments).

The culture of the school encourages experimentation. Experiments are discussed, improved, and tried again, not unlike the plan-do-check-improve process described by Total Quality Management participants (Deming, 1986). Principal Eric Nadelstern provides this rationale for International's collaborative work on instruction:

You have to engage people in conversation about what they're doing. Focus on how to do it better, and give them the opportunity to work on it together. Implement it, reflect on it, work with these experiences, and take it to the next level. So what winds up happening is that you're also modeling the pedagogy. It's kind of a discovery approach to learning. You begin to approach it in both ways: Analyze the experience as learners while the content is pedagogy. (personal communication, February 3, 1994)

The results of this process were diffused to all staff by the connections among peer groups and committees, faculty presentations, summer staff development institutes, and informal visiting among classrooms. These exchanges also benefit from the varied expertise of the faculty: Teachers with backgrounds in ESL, bilingual education, and other content areas supplement each other's strengths, as more and more information is shared over the years. Further, the school has an explicit policy to document its practices and approaches in writing, in part due to its active participation in fund-raising activities. Proposals, handbooks, curriculum guides, and a school journal have added other means of sharing ideas about teaching and learning among the staff (see, for example, Ancess & Darling-Hammond, 1994; Heisler, Rugger, & Slater, 1987-88; Hirschy, 1990; International High School, 1987-88, n.d.; Rugger, 1990).

Interdisciplinary team teaching
International's collaborative arrangements have continued to deepen as the school has matured. In the past few years, the faculty has restructured the school to emphasize interdisciplinary teams as the fundamental staff grouping of the organization. In 1990, four teachers developed a new course called *Motion,* in which physics, math, English, and physical education were all studied under the general rubric of the theme of motion. Structurally, this "interdisciplinary cluster course" differed from regular singleton courses in that a group of approximately 25 students would remain together for an entire 13-week term, while the four teachers met regularly to integrate their activities around motion and discuss student performance. As these teachers compared the performance and engagement of the students in the cluster course to those in their singleton classes, they found that cluster students were performing significantly better. They attribute this to the integrated nature of the curriculum, which they feel made the

material more interesting, as well as to the social climate that was created by the more intensive interactions among students and between students and faculty. *Motion* was subsequently offered to more students over the following terms, and in a short time cluster courses proliferated, as other teachers began offering their own interdisciplinary themes.

After intensive faculty deliberation during the 1992-93 school year, the school converted in September 1993 to a comprehensive interdisciplinary curriculum. Six faculty teams of four to seven staff members each offer two cluster courses during the academic year, comprising a total of 12 different theme clusters from which students may choose. Students select one cluster each term, and teams are then provided with rooms and planning time to build a curriculum in an autonomous fashion, subject to the pedagogical norms that have been developed in the school over the years. These teams thus constitute the central organizational staff grouping of the school. They assume the primary responsibility for hiring new members and introducing them to the practices of the school as well as for assessing and developing the skills of their members. Individuals from other teams also sit on hiring committees and tenure-review committees, so that a fresh perspective is added to the discussion. Each team sends a representative to a coordinating council, which determines the policy direction of the school, subject to approval of the entire faculty on major decisions. Teachers regard the all-school interdisciplinary structure as surprisingly successful. They remain committed to their team organization, having found the initial results observed by the *Motion* team to have been replicated as the model has expanded. Thus far, measures of student outcomes remain generally at the level of those of the past, and in several cases have begun to improve as the faculty continue with the restructuring effort.

Small-group student collaboration
The reciprocal interaction between the way teacher groups and student groups work is widely acknowledged throughout the school's publica-

tions and conversations. An excerpt from the teacher-written personnel manual observes:

> If we view ourselves to be true educators, we must also view ourselves as learners. We are role models for our students. If we model authority, our students will learn to be authoritarian. If we model self-improvement in an atmosphere of sharing, that is what our students will learn. (International High School: *Personnel Procedures for Peer Selection, Support and Evaluation*, p. 5)

Teachers explicitly draw an analogy between the philosophy and expectations that underlie student work groups and their own collaborative peer evaluation, staff development, and administrative processes. Student groups have been structured in ways that parallel staff committees; student portfolios followed teacher portfolios as a means of assessment in many classes; and evaluation processes for students mirror those used for teachers.

Like the gradual evolution of faculty collaboration, the faculty's experimentation with cooperative learning also began slowly. In the early stages, group work was introduced by individual teachers in circumscribed ways within a traditional curriculum. Administrators and visiting teachers would then discuss how to expand those activities, so that what began as several student groups working on the same projects diversified to groups doing different projects. Then teachers experimented with ways to make the presentation of one group to another more active for the audience, using viewer guides and evaluation schemas. Now teachers use portfolios, student conferences, group-to-group exchanges, and a variety of other mechanisms to avoid simply replacing teacher lectures with student group lectures.

Teachers usually divide students into multilingual groups to encourage students to speak English with one another. Novice English speakers are typically paired with intermediate English speakers. The underlying philosophy is that students learn language skills and conceptual material better when surrounded by a great variety of comprehensible or barely comprehensible language input, especially when given the opportunity to practice their own output by conversing or writing in a range of contexts throughout the day.

Students usually begin research for their group projects—such as the creation of a newspaper or a book on Mesopotamian culture—by looking at the projects created by other students in the past. From these past projects, they not only learn content, but are enabled to see that the work of students (both those in the past and their own) is valued and respected.

English and native language learning through content

In addition to the organizational and curricular characteristics of International, the faculty also follow a number of pedagogical principles they have developed over the years as they have adapted to the specific needs of new immigrants to the United States. The thrust of the concept of "language through content" is that learning proceeds best when the relevance and use of information and skills are made clear by connecting them to a context in which they are applied. Ideas take on a preeminent status according to this philosophy, as students are encouraged to become adult thinkers, a process they further by developing linguistic skills to aid in the expression of their thoughts.

Rooted in the linguistic notion that comprehension precedes production, this approach has the implication that students who do not yet speak English well can nonetheless begin to grapple with conceptual ideas, especially if they have been exposed to such material in their native language. Native language development is encouraged, particularly in a couple of clusters, by allowing some student groupings to be homogeneous in terms of native language, especially when students are working on projects related to their native culture. Moreover, the focus on content has the added advantage that teachers come to know their students' strengths and weaknesses in English and to understand some of the conceptual differences that students grapple with as they are exposed to an American curriculum. Teachers have cited examples such as Western ideas of linearity and narration as ideas that students from some cultures have difficulties with. These are concepts that cannot be reduced to simple matters of language comprehension.

Principles underlying teacher work

An example of International's integration of collaborative instructional planning, activity-based cooperative learning, and language through content is found in the way the teacher teams come together to create the activity guides that form the foundations of each team's curriculum. Activity guides replace lesson plans at the school and lay out student tasks in accessible English. Teachers assemble supporting materials, such as stories or directions for a physics experiment, in such a way that the linguistic load is minimized. With the goal of doing justice to the essential idea under consideration, teachers rewrite more difficult texts in accessible English or use core excerpts from longer texts to build an activity, using graphic organizers when possible. Over time, teams develop a greater variety of activity guides and provide more choice to students in selecting the order in which they pursue the projects they will complete during a term. At times, teachers allow a group of students to translate texts into their native language if they feel this will aid understanding. Teachers new to International usually require considerable coaching as they attempt to construct activity guides that allow students to be actively involved in the learning process, (i.e., that are not simply teacher-written workbooks) and that are written in language that is accessible to the students.

Finally, the staff development process at International follows a few rules of thumb to guide teachers in their instructional planning and delivery. For instance, "start at the beginning" suggests that assignments be explained first by not assuming student familiarity with matters that would be obvious to U.S. students, such as how to use a book. "Break down the task" implies that the two-to three-week projects that students often work on be broken down into smaller segments, each of which is demonstrated with an example before students themselves carry out the task. One teacher tells of an elaborate process over several weeks in which students read book chapters, wrote reading logs, exchanged reading logs with other students, reread texts, wrote draft book reports, exchanged these reports, practiced delivering reports in pairs, and created audience guides in preparation for a day when they would present their much-practiced reports to an audience already somewhat familiar with their contents. A third rule of thumb recommends that teachers model examples of finished products of assignments as well as the process that leads to the finished product. This practice is described in a teacher-written handbook:

If students are assigned to write journals, then the teacher should write his/her journal on the chalkboard *while the students watch.* In an interviewing project, the students need to be shown how to create questions before they are required to create their own. A way to do this is to list all the items they want to know about their interviewees (e.g., name, language, occupation, residence, hobbies). Then discuss point by point what questions to ask in order to get the desired information. Then the students can develop their own questions, and finally, they can put the questions in a logical sequence. (International High School, 1993, pp. 5-6)

Other rules of thumb differ from teaching practices that are sometimes recommended for native English speakers: repeating teacher questions several times, repeating student responses, and writing on the chalkboard, even if that means one's back is turned to the students. International's strategies for incorporating successful practices into explicit guidance for teachers and students are combined with collaborative teaching and staff development opportunities to create shared standards for practice throughout the school.

The Bilingual Cooperative Integrated Reading and Composition (BCIRC) Model

The Bilingual Cooperative Integrated Reading and Composition Model is used in a number of schools and districts around the country. Based on a cooperative learning model developed at Johns Hopkins University, it creates a context that facilitates high-quality interactions for bilingual and language minority students. Students experience extensive opportunities to use oral language to express ideas, exchange information, and build comprehension for literacy development. Literacy skills are practiced and developed through literature and the content areas.

The BCIRC model blends cooperative and independent learning strategies using teacher-directed and partner-supported activities. Its constructivist approach to second language acquisition is adaptable to various grade levels and program options. It is used in middle and high schools for teaching ESL and sheltered social studies, math, and science. It is also used in elementary schools for transitional bilingual language arts programs because of its strength in creating a natural transition between second language reading and writing skills. BCIRC lends itself to curriculum integration and is used in elementary schools as a "reading across the curriculum" model for content-area reading in a second language. Finally, it is useful in two-way bilingual programs, because students learn through discussion, reading, and writing in two languages, with peers who are more proficient in English.

The program holds a strong philosophy of equity, quality, and high expectations for all learners, including administrators, teachers, parents, and students. It views learning as a social enterprise; thus cooperative learning is seen as an integral part of literacy, social, and cognitive development. Elements of collegial learning, coaching, collaborative decision making, planning, and ongoing assessment and improvement pervade all aspects of the educational landscape where BCIRC is in use. Students engage in processes of team formation and team building; the development of social and cooperative norms; vocabulary building in the context of oral, silent, and peer reading strategies; debriefing strategies for content, learning and thinking processes, and social behavior; and strategies for formulating and answering questions, reading and writing for comprehension and expression, and self- and peer evaluation.

Teacher learning communities

In BCIRC, professional development focuses on interaction among teachers in the same way that classroom activities focus on interaction among students. Teachers learn by interacting with more capable peers as well as university faculty and consultants (Calderón, 1990-91; Fullan, 1991; Tharp & Gallimore, 1989). Professional development in the BCIRC model is "a continuous blend of workshops, follow-up collaborative reflection, application, fine-tuning, new workshops, reflection, [and] application" that builds on the "richness and diversity of the teachers and their experiences" (Calderón, 1994a, p. 21).

In teacher learning communities (TLCs), teachers identify areas of interest, problems, and solutions; plan and organize their professional development activities; share knowledge, teaching skills, and student products; and conduct peer observations and coaching. TLC meetings can occur anywhere in the school. For instance, sixth-grade teachers from the Harris Middle School in the San Antonio (Texas) Independent School District selected their science lab as the home for their TLC. Each day of the week has a different focus. For instance, on one day the TLC may discuss curriculum. Another day is devoted to speaking with the principal and taking care of school business. On the third day, the teachers may study articles and further their knowledge base, and on the fourth day they may work to solve problems that individual students are having. They may use the last day of the week to catch up on unfinished business and celebrate the accomplishments of the week. Typical activities described by Calderón (1994a, pp. 23-26) include the following:

- Joint study of theory, philosophy, and research on each area of innovation teachers are working on: Teachers read articles from journals in a jigsaw fashion. They teach each other the part of the article that they have. Afterwards, they discuss the implications and relevance of the article to their own situations.
- Peer demonstrations of teaching strategies: Teachers demonstrate and provide sample scripts of questions they use to analyze content, cooperative skills, and learning strategies.
- Analysis and discussion of how to adapt teaching to meet diverse student needs: Teachers discuss, for example, how a teacher with only

a few language minority students in class adapts and modifies a classroom activity to ensure student success.

- Discussion of peer coaching or mentoring in support of an innovation: Teachers design instruments to observe the implementation of new strategies and processes.

- Practice in giving and receiving technical feedback: Teachers watch videos of other teachers outside of the group and role play giving feedback. Teachers also get feedback from peer coaches, mentors, or university faculty to strengthen their practices.

- Joint analysis of video recordings of teaching and learning: Teachers share an instructional segment with colleagues, then discuss successes and areas for improvement.

- Adaptation of curriculum: Interdisciplinary units receive continuous development and refinement.

- Analysis of student portfolios, assessment processes, work samples, and test results: Teachers analyze evidence of student growth, discuss implications for instruction, and identify target strategies and goals.

- Reflection, decision making, and professional development around areas of concern: Teachers plan and organize professional development activities and types of support needed for particular problems.

- Organization of workshops and classroom demonstrations for other teachers.

- Meetings with teachers from students' home cultures to learn more about bilingual instruction and to further their bilingual–bicultural knowledge and skills: Teachers meet with other teachers to exchange ideas, practice communicating with colleagues in another language, and learn more about their students' backgrounds.

The BCIRC TLC model illustrates how integrating cooperative learning, collective research, and reflective strategies can facilitate the professional development of teachers of immigrant students.

Effectiveness of the approach

Research on BCIRC schools and classrooms has documented the effectiveness of both the general approach to teaching it supports and the strategies for teacher development it has engendered (Calderón, 1994b). Bilingual students in BCIRC programs

- have a greater variety of second language practice opportunities through natural corrections from their peers and the development of their own self-correction devices through frequent analyses of their teaching;
- experience higher levels of linguistic and information processing accuracy because of their constant interaction with native speakers of other languages;
- view their own language as having status, which results in high self-esteem and a belief that bilingualism is an asset rather than a deficit;
- understand the global implications of literacy as well as the implications of literacy in each language and culture;
- use the whole range of their first-language capabilities in learning English; and
- learn important life skills for working in multinational and multiethnic contexts.

The most promising staff development practices associated with BCIRC programs include attention to (1) school contexts for teacher development; (2) stages that teachers go through when implementing cooperative learning models; (3) the content and processes of effective learning activities, including how cooperative learning strategies can be used as professional development tools; and (4) the ways that teachers construct learning communities for continuous improvement, including how they become both researchers and curriculum developers by working together.

When implementing cooperative learning, mainstream classroom teachers experience personal and professional changes as they integrate new teaching approaches into their repertoire, use new materials, alter their beliefs and pedagogical assumptions, and incorporate new classroom norms into their teaching processes. In addition, bilingual teachers experience change as they develop proficiency in teaching in two languages and in using new approaches that address students' varying levels of linguistic and conceptual thinking. These changes require ongoing daily support if they are to be fully realized.

Calderón (1994a) reports that teacher inservice training must be linked to processes for renewal and follow-up support if it is to be successful in changing classroom practice. In the BCIRC model, a number of strategies proved to be important. For example, teachers benefited from presentations about the theory of, philosophy of, and research on cooperative learning, literacy development, and alternative assessment when the presentations were followed by extensive observation by teachers of BCIRC teaching models conducted in both languages as well as analysis and discussion of how to adapt teaching to meet diverse student needs. Activities for developing teachers' and students' cooperative skills were also useful, along with protocols and guided practice to support peer coaching, mentoring, and interactive peer journals. Teachers learned from video analysis and reflection on their own teaching performances and decisions as well as the study and analysis of student performance through alternative assessments and portfolios. They profited from having time to work on adapting school curriculum and lessons to student needs and from self-directed collaborative study groups, where they could work with colleagues to refine their practices and deal with problems.

This program, like the others we have described, illustrates several principles for successful professional development.

- Teachers need occasions to connect theory and practice in tightly integrated ways.
- Teachers need support in learning to look closely at students to understand what they bring to the classroom.

- Teachers benefit from concrete strategies for shaping hands-on, collaborative learning environments that build on students' language, culture, and experience.
- Teachers appreciate and use ongoing opportunities for collaboration and collective problem solving.
- Teachers profit from experiences that allow them to learn and work professionally in the same ways that they hope to teach.

Building preparation programs and school learning communities that provide these kinds of opportunities for teachers is one of the most important investments society can make in the education of immigrant youth.

Conclusion

In this volume we have discussed the historical background of diversity in the United States and the evolution of beliefs and values that underlie current policies relative to immigrant education. We have stressed the interpersonal aspect of education in the context of social diversity, especially in the education of immigrant youth, where students and teachers may not speak the same language. We have also emphasized that speakers of languages other than English who live in the United States have identities and intellectual capacities that teachers need to understand and build on. When viewing teacher preservice and inservice professional development through this lens, looking at the *people* who inhabit the classrooms and who work very hard to do what they think is best, it is possible to look beyond the traditional staff development model for examples of program designs that will preserve the dignity of and improve possibilities for both professional educators and their students.

The programs profiled illustrate exemplary practices in professional development for teachers of immigrant youth. Though no one program employs all the structures and practices outlined in this volume, all exhibit at least some of them. Below we summarize three themes that run through the volume—the social and cyclical nature of learning, the need for an anthropological orientation in understanding students and the teachers who work with them, and the promise of video and other technology to help school staff view and reflect on their work.

The Social and Cyclical Nature of Learning

Whether professional development for teachers of immigrant students takes place in preservice or inservice programs, the conceptual explication and strategies that promote dialogue and reflection among teachers follow common patterns. For example, cooperative learning, problem-based inquiry (including action research), peer coaching, cognitive coaching, team teaching, school–home collaboration, teacher-initiated research, teacher-initiated curriculum writing, developmental and reflective approaches to supervision, and microteaching using video technology all operate from the premise that learning is a social and cyclical process (see the table below). What we know about good learning environments for students applies to teachers as well. Professional development packaged in a transmission approach inhibits the interaction that builds community and increases teacher capac-

Strategies to Promote Dialogue and Reflection

Strategy	Process	Interactional Approach	Objective
Cognitive Coaching	Be aware of the problem. Identify possible causes of the problem. Suggest alternative solutions. Select a solution. Assess outcomes.	Directive, nondirective, and collaborative interactions	Building trust and problem-solving skills
Peer Coaching	Study Demonstration Practice and feedback Coaching	Collegial problem solving	Collegiality; implementation skills
Action Research	Problem formulation Data collection Data analysis Reporting of results Action planning	Collaborative, participatory	Organizational reflection
Micro-teaching	Limited/bundled skills focus Scaled-down video segments (5-10 minutes) Maximum feedback to assist self-evaluation Live or videotaped perceptual model Positive reinforcement	Nondirective counseling approach by trainer	Individual technical improvement

ity. Traditional workshop-focused staff development places adult learners in the position of passive recipients of knowledge, delivered by an expert. We propose a more interactive approach that encourages adults to create their own knowledge as they grow professionally.

The cyclical pattern of interactive development through group learning involves visiting and revisiting questions about practice, collecting and interpreting data, revising hypotheses, and changing practice in light of new knowledge. This pattern is an integral part of the structures, practices, concepts, and principles that guide the composition of this volume, and it is evident in the examples of actual practice in preservice and inservice programs.

Anthropological Orientations

Because misunderstandings about students and teachers often find their source in language and cultural differences, an anthropological orientation to professional development is appropriate. Teachers and other school staff need to understand that language difference does not mean communication deficit and that cultural differences are not problems that need to be remedied. When teachers and other school staff examine—from an anthropological perspective—themselves, the community they serve, the learning community in the school, and the relationships of these entities with one another, they begin to understand more deeply the wealth possessed by the newest members of the community. They can become a part of that community, rather than an observer or a technical worker who leaves it at the end of the work day.

An anthropological approach interacts with and complements the group-oriented professional development program designs we have described. Gathering qualitative data in the context of teacher-initiated research, for instance, places the teacher at the center of the research loop. As the teacher works through and begins to interpret data with colleagues, the dialogue begins and richer interpretations are possible, because more than one person acts as interpreter. This is the beginning of a collegial community of educators. The contributions of other educators add additional data and insight to the initiator's research. Feedback can be processed by the group, applied to the setting, and evaluated, and initial questions can be revised or resolved. From this process, teachers improve their capacity to make sound judgments about the interaction between their own practice and the students in their classes, with an aim toward improving the former and providing optimal learning opportunities for the latter.

Another point emphasized in this volume is the importance of reciprocity and mutuality in the education of immigrant students. If teachers are to respect and value the identities and abilities of their students, designers of professional development programs must respect and value teachers' identities and abilities as well. It is extremely important to work closely and over long periods of time with teachers and other school leaders to develop the deep relationships that will support this difficult, often uncomfortable work.

Technological Applications

Finally, we have suggested the use of video technology to support professional development activities focused around microteaching lessons. Using video technology to examine practice for the purpose of professional growth is hardly a new development. Microteaching was first studied at Stanford University in 1963 (Pack, 1970). This dormant feature of the professional development landscape shows exquisite promise in the last years of this century and into the next one. More research on the use of videoethnographic and computer techniques to support professional development for teachers of immigrant students is indicated.

The programs profiled to illustrate exemplary practice were selected because they exemplify these three dimensions of professional development design: the use of strategies that are compatible with their settings and supported by compatible policy; the practice of viewing community anthropologically; and the use of technology to support microteaching to help teachers and other school leaders see themselves more objectively. Where a few of these components are present, there will be some professional growth among participants. Where many or all are present, professional growth promises to be of longer duration and profoundly articulated in practice. These concepts promise to address the challenges in the educational arena in which the student population is increasingly diverse and teachers need to meet this diversity head-on in their classrooms. These concepts point to professional development designs that are close to where practitioners work and that foster collaboration among teachers within the learning communities of which they are part. Finally, such professional development designs can forge strong collaborative relationships between schools and other agencies, such as universities, that can provide technical support in school-based research. The greater the number of partners, the richer the breadth of knowledge for practitioners as they work together to improve the educational experience of all students, including immigrants.

Much more could be said about each of the programs, ideas, and practices mentioned here. This volume is a springboard for discussion among educators who are encountering increasing linguistic diversity and larger numbers of immigrant students in their classrooms. It can serve as a focal point for discussion about how to enhance their understanding of immigrant students. It can also provide the basis for reflection and dialogue on their own beliefs about the meaning of being an immigrant and the interaction between these beliefs and professional practice. New designs for the professional development of teachers of immigrant youth promise exciting educational opportunities for immigrant youth as well.

References

Alexander, P.A., & Dochy, F.J.R.C. (1995). Conceptions of knowledge and beliefs: A comparison across varying cultural and educational communities. *American Educational Research Journal, 32*(2), 413-442.

Alexander, W.M., & George, P.S. (1981). *The exemplary middle school.* New York: Holt, Rinehart & Winston.

Ancess, J., & Darling-Hammond, L. (1994). *Authentic teaching, learning, and assessment with new English learners at International High School.* New York: Columbia University, Teachers College, National Center for Restructuring Education, Schools, and Teaching.

Anyon, J. (1980). Social class and the hidden curriculum of work. *Journal of Education, 162,* 67-92.

Apple, M., & King, N. (1983). What do schools teach? In H. Giroux & D. Purpel (Eds.), *The hidden curriculum and moral education: Deception or discovery?* (pp. 82-99). Berkeley, CA: McCutchan.

August, D., & García, E. (1988). *Language minority education in the United States: Research, policy and practice.* Springfield, IL: C.C. Thomas.

Bailey, M.A. (1993). Bilingual education: Legal perspectives and policy considerations. *Illinois Schools Journal, 72*(2), 33-39.

Banks, J. (1984). *Teaching strategies for ethnic studies* (3rd ed.). Boston: Allyn & Bacon.

Berryman, S.E., & Bailey, T.R. (1992). *The double helix of education and the economy.* New York: Columbia University, Teachers College, Institute on Education and the Economy.

Bowers, C.A., & Flinders, D.J. (1990). *Responsive teaching: An ecological approach to classroom patterns of language, culture, and thought.* New York: Teachers College Press.

Bowers, C.A., & Flinders, D.J. (1991). *Culturally responsive teaching and supervision: A handbook for staff development.* New York: Teachers College Press.

Brimelow, P. (1995). *Alien nation: Common sense about America's immigration disaster.* New York: Random House.

Brinton, D.M., Snow, M.A., & Wesche, M.B. (1989). *Content-based second language instruction.* New York: Newbury House.

Bryk, A.S., & Driscoll, M.E. (1988). The high school as community: Contextual influences and consequences for students and teachers. Madison, WI: National Center on Effective Secondary Schools. (ERIC Document Reproduction Service No. ED 302 539)

Calderón, M. (1990-91). Cooperative learning builds communities of teachers. *Teacher Education and Practice: The Journal of the Texas Association of Colleges for Teacher Education, 6*(2) 75-77.

Calderón, M. (1994a). *Bilingual teacher development within school learning communities: A synthesis of the staff development model* (Research report). Baltimore, MD: Johns Hopkins University Center for Research on Education for Students at Risk.

Calderón, M. (1994b). Cooperative learning for bilingual settings. In R. Rodríguez, N.J. Ramos, & J.A. Ruiz-Escalante (Eds.), *Compendium of readings in bilingual education: Issues and practices* (pp. 95-110). San Antonio: The Texas Association for Bilingual Education.

Calderón, M. (1995, April). *Dual language programs and team-teachers' professional development.* Paper presented at the annual meeting of the American Educational Research Association, San Francisco.

Carnevale, A.P. (1991). *America and the new economy: How new competitive standards are radically changing America's workplaces.* San Francisco: Jossey-Bass.

Carter, T.P., & Chatfield, M.L. (1986). Effective bilingual schools: Implications for policy and practice. *American Journal of Education, 5,* 200-234.

Cascio, C. (1995). National Board for Professional Teaching Standards: Changing teaching through teachers. *Clearing House, 68*(4), 211-213.

Chavez, L. (1994). Preface: The new immigrant challenge. In J. Miller (Ed.), *Strangers at our gate* (pp. 5-8). Washington, DC: The Manhattan Institute.

Clair, N. (1993). *Beliefs, self-reported practices and professional development needs of three classroom teachers with language-minority students.* Unpublished doctoral dissertation, Teachers College, Columbia University, New York.

Clark, D.L., & Meloy, J.M. (1990). Recanting bureaucracy: A democratic structure for leadership in schools. In A. Lieberman (Ed.), *Schools as collaborative cultures: Creating the future now* (pp. 3-23). New York: Teachers College Press.

Collier, V. (1987). Age and rate of acquisition of second language for academic purposes. *TESOL Quarterly, 21,* 617-41.

Costa, A.L., & Garmston, R. (1985). Supervision for intelligent teaching. *Educational Leadership, 42*(5), 70-80.

Costa, A.L., & Garmston, R. (1986). Cognitive coaching: Supervision for intelligent teaching. *Wingspan, 3*(1).

Costa, A.L., & Kallick, B. (1993). Through the lens of a critical friend. *Educational Leadership, 51*(2), 49-51.

Cotton, K. (1987). Reducing teacher turnover in reservation schools: A guide for administrators. Portland, OR: Northwest Regional Educational Laboratory. (ERIC Document Reproduction Service No. ED 288 686)

Crandall, J.A. (1993). Content-centered learning in the United States. *Annual Review of Applied Linguisitcs, 13*, 111-126.

Cummins, J. (1986). Empowering minority students: A framework for intervention. In J. Kretovics (Ed.), *Transforming urban education* (pp. 327-346). Boston: Allyn and Bacon.

Darling-Hammond, L. (1986). A proposal for evaluation in the teaching profession. *Elementary school journal, 86*(4), 1-21.

Darling-Hammond, L. (1990). Teacher professionalism: Why and how. In A. Lieberman (Ed.), *Schools as collaborative cultures: Creating the future now* (pp. 25-50). New York: The Falmer Press.

Darling-Hammond, L. (1993). Reframing the school reform agenda: Developing capacity for school transformation. *Phi Delta Kappan, 74*, 752-761.

Darling-Hammond, L. (1994a). Developing professional development schools: Early Lessons, Challenge, and Promise. In L. Darling-Hammond (Ed.), *Professional development schools: Schools for developing a profession* (pp. 1-27). New York: Teachers College Press.

Darling-Hammond, L. (1994b). Standards for teachers. 34th Charles W. Hunt Memorial Lecture. Paper presented at the Annual Meeting of the American Association of Colleges for Teacher Education, Chicago. (ERIC Document Reproduction Service No. ED 378 176)

Darling-Hammond, L., Ancess, J., & Falk, B. (1995). *Authentic assessment in action: Studies of schools and students at work.* New York: Teachers College Press.

Darling-Hammond, L., & McLaughlin, M. (1995). Policies that support professional development in an era of reform. *Phi Delta Kappan, 76*, 597-604.

Darling-Hammond, L., Snyder, J., Ancess, J., Einbender, L., Goodwin, A.L., & MacDonald, M. (1993). *Creating learner-centered accountability.* New York: Columbia University, Teachers College, National Center for Restructuring Education, Schools, and Teaching.

Decker, R.H., & Dedrick, C.V.L. (1989). Peer mentoring exchange program: Opportunities for professional improvement. (ERIC Document Reproduction Service No. ED 317 347)

Deming, W.E. (1986). *Out of the crisis.* Cambridge, MA: MIT Press.

Drucker, P. (1989). The new realities: In government and politics, in economics and business, in society and world view. New York: Harper and Row.

Elam, S., Rose, L., & Gallup, A. (1994). *Gallup poll of the public's attitudes toward the public schools.* Princeton, NJ: The Gallup Organization.

Falk, B., MacMurdy, S., & Darling-Hammond, L. (1995). *Taking a different look: How the primary language record supports teaching for diverse learners.* New York: Columbia University, Teachers College, National Center for Restructuring Education, Schools, and Teaching.

Freire, P. (1970). *Pedagogy of the oppressed.* New York: Continuum.

Fullan, M. (1991). *The new meaning of educational change.* New York: Teachers College Press.

García, E. (1989). Instructional discourse in "effective" Hispanic classrooms. In R. Jacobson & C. Faltis (Eds.), *Language distribution issues in bilingual schooling* (pp. 104-120). Clevedon, England: Multilingual Matters.

García, E. (1993). Language, culture and education. In L. Darling-Hammond (Ed.), *Review of Research in Education, 19* (pp. 51-98). Washington, DC: American Educational Research Association.

Garman, N.B. (1986). Reflection, the heart of clinical supervision: A modern rationale for practice. *Journal of Curriculum and Supervision, 2*(1), 1-24.

Gomez, M.L., & Tabachnik, B.R. (1992). Telling teaching stories. *Teaching Education, 4,* 129-138.

González, J. (1993). School meanings and cultural bias. *Education and Urban Society, 25,* 254-269.

González, J. (1994). Bilingual education: A review of policy and ideologies. In R. Rodríguez, N.J. Ramos, & J.A. Ruiz-Escalante (Eds.), *Compendium of readings in bilingual education: Issues and practices.* San Antonio: The Texas Association for Bilingual Education.

González, J.M., & Szecsy, E.M. (Eds.). (1997). *New limits for new times: A cyber-symposium* [CD-ROM]. New York: Columbia University, Teachers College, National Center for Restructuring Education, Schools, and Teaching.

Grant, C.A., & Zeichner, K.M. (1984). On becoming a reflective teacher. In C.A. Grant (Ed.), *Preparing for reflective teaching* (pp. 1-18). Boston: Allyn & Bacon.

Gray, L., Cahalan, M., Hein, S., Litman, C., Severynse, J., Warren, S., Wisan, G., & Stowe, P. (1993). *New teachers in the job market, 1991 update* (NCES 93-392). Washington, DC: U.S. Department of Education, Office of Educational Research and Improvement.

Hakuta, K. (1986). *Mirror of language.* New York: Basic Books.

Harris (Louis) & Associates, Inc. (1991). *Coming to terms: Teachers' views on current issues in education: The Metropolitan Life Survey of the American Teacher, 1991.* (Available from Metropolitan Life Insurance Company, Teachers' Survey 1991, One Madison Avenue, New York NY 10010-3690) (ERIC Document Reproduction Service No. ED 334 168)

Heisler, D., Rugger, K., & Slater, M. (1987-1988). English. In *Beyond high school graduation requirements: What do students need to learn at The International High School?* Long Island City, NY: The International High School.

Hersh, S.B., Stroot, S., & Snyder, M. (1993, April). *Mentoring entry year teachers in rural communities: A model program.* Paper presented at the Annual Meeting of the American Educational Research Association, Atlanta. (ERIC Document Reproduction Service No. ED 362 352)

Hirschy, D. (1990). The new schedule. In *Insights: Thoughts on the process of being International* (pp. 6-9). Long Island City, NY: The International High School.

Howey, K.R., & Zimpher, N.L. (1993). *Patterns in prospective teachers: Guides for designing preservice programs.* Unpublished manuscript, Ohio State University.

Huling-Austin, L., & Murphy, S.C. (1987). *Assessing the impact of teacher induction programs: Implications for program development.* Paper presented at the Annual meeting of the American Educational Research Association, Washington, DC.

Igoa, C. (1995). *The inner world of the immigrant child.* New York: St. Martin's Press.

Immigrant Policy Project, State and Local Coalition on Immigration. (1995, December). Much of Prop. 187 Struck Down. *Immigrant Policy News: The State–Local Report, 2*(2), 1-2.

International High School at LaGuardia Community College. (n.d.). *Educational philosophy.* Long Island City, NY: Author.

International High School at LaGuardia Community College. (n.d.). *Personnel procedures for peer selection, support and evaluation.* Long Island City, NY: Author.

International High School at LaGuardia Community College, The Curriculum Committee. (1987-1988). *Beyond high school graduation requirements: What do students need to learn at the International High School?* Long Island City, NY: Author.

International High School at LaGuardia Community College. (1993). *Project PROPEL handbook: Resources for adopting sites.* Long Island City, NY: Author.

Jackson, P.W. (1983). The daily grind .... In H. Giroux & D. Purpel (Eds.), *The hidden curriculum and moral education: Deception or discovery?* (pp. 28-60). Berkeley, CA: McCutchan. (Original work published 1968)

Jackson, S. (1992). *Autobiography: Pivot points for the study and practice of multiculturalism in teacher education.* Paper presented at the annual meeting of the American Educational Research Association, San Francisco.

Joyce, B., & Showers, B. (1982). The coaching of teaching. *Educational Leadership, 40*(1), 4-10.

Joyce, B., & Showers, B. (1988). *Student achievement through staff development.* New York: Longman.

Kagan, S. (1993). The structural approach to cooperative learning. In D.D. Holt (Ed.), *Cooperative learning: A response to linguistic and cultural diversity* (pp. 9-17). McHenry, IL and Washington, DC: Delta Systems and Center for Applied Linguistics.

King, J. (1991). Dysconscious racism: Ideology, identity, and the miseducation of teachers. *The Journal of Negro Education, 60,* 133-146.

King, J., & Ladson-Billings, G. (1990). The teacher education challenge in elite university settings: Developing critical perspectives for teaching in a democratic and multicultural society. *European Journal of Intercultural Studies, 1,* 15-30.

Kloss, H. (in press). *The American bilingual tradition.* McHenry, IL and Washington, DC: Delta Systems and Center for Applied Linguistics. (Original work published 1977)

Kohlberg, L. (1983). The moral atmosphere of the school. In H. Giroux & D. Purpel (Eds.), *The hidden curriculum and moral education: Deception or discovery?* (pp. 61-81). Berkeley, CA: McCutchan. (Original work published 1970)

Knowles, M. (1980). *The modern practice of adult education.* Englewood Cliffs, NJ: Cambridge Adult Education.

Krashen, S.D. (1985). *Input hypothesis: Issues and implications.* New York: Longman.

Kuhlman, N.A., & Vidal, J. (1993). Meeting the needs of LEP students through new teacher training: The case in California. *The Journal of Educational Issues of Language Minority Students, 12,* 97-113.

Ladson-Billings, G. (1995). Multicultural teacher education: Research, practice, and policy. In J. Banks & C. Banks (Eds.), *Handbook on research on Multicultural education* (pp. 747-59). New York: Macmillan.

Leibowitz, A.H. (1982). Federal recognition of the rights of minority language groups. Rosslyn, VA: National Clearinghouse for Bilingual Education.

Lieberman, A. (1995). *The work of restructuring schools.* New York: Teachers College Press.

Lieberman, A., & McLaughlin, M. (1992). Networks for educational change: powerful and problematic. *Phi Delta Kappan, 73,* 673-677.

Lieberman, A., & Miller, L. (1992). Teacher development in professional practice schools. In M. Levine (Ed.), *Professional practice schools: Linking teacher education and school reform* (pp. 105-123). New York: Teachers College Press.

Little, J.W. (1993). *Teachers' professional development in a climate of educational reform.* New York: Columbia University, Teachers College, National Center for Restructuring Education, Schools, and Teaching.

Little, J.W., & McLaughlin, M.W. (1991). *Urban math collaboratives: As teachers tell it.* Stanford, CA: Center for Research on the Context of Secondary School Teaching.

Lucas, T. (1993). What have we learned from research on successful secondary programs for LEP students? A synthesis of findings from three studies. *Proceedings of the Third National Research Symposium on Limited English Proficient Student Issues: Focus on middle and high school issues, Vol. 1* (pp. 81-111). Washington, DC: U.S. Department of Education, Office of Bilingual Education and Minority Languages Affairs.

Lucas, T., Henze, R., & Donato, R. (1990). Promoting the success of Latino language minority students: An exploratory study of six high schools. *Harvard Educational Review, 60,* 315-340.

Lucas, T., & Schecter, S.R. (1992). Literacy education and diversity: Toward equity in the teaching of reading and writing. *The Urban Review, 24*(2), pp. 85-104.

Lyons, J.J. (1990, March). The past and future directions of federal bilingual-education policy. *Annals of the American Academy of Political and Social Science*, pp. 66-80.

Macdonald, J. (1983). Curriculum, consciousness, and social change. In H. Giroux & D. Purpel (Eds.), *The hidden curriculum and moral education: Deception or discovery?* (pp. 292-308). Berkeley, CA: McCutchan. (Original work published 1981)

Macdonald, M., & Szecsy, E. (1996, April). A network for equity: Advocacy, biliteracy, and technology at Haverstraw Middle School. In A. Lieberman (Chair/Discussant), *Networking in support of systemic reform in a context of diversity: Inter- and intradistrict collaborations in the Dewey Network*. Symposium conducted at the Annual Meeting of the American Educational Research Association, New York.

McIntosh, P. (1989, July/August). White privilege: Unpacking the invisible knapsack. *Peace and Freedom*.

McLaughlin, M.W. (1991). Enabling professional development: What have we learned? In A. Lieberman & L. Miller (Eds.), *Staff development for education in the '90s*, (2nd ed.) (pp. 61-82). New York: Teachers College Press.

Miller, E. (1995). Shared decision-making by itself doesn't make for better decisions. *The Harvard Education Letter, 11*(6), 1-4.

Miller, L. (1992). Curriculum work as staff development. In W. Pink & A. Hyde (Eds.), *Effective staff development for change* (pp. 95-109). Norwood, NJ: Ablex.

Miller, L., & Silvernail, D. (1994). Wells Junior High School: Evolution of a professional development school. In L. Darling-Hammond (Ed.), *Professional development schools: Schools for developing a profession* (pp. 28-49). New York: Teachers College Press.

Minicucci, C., & Olsen, L. (1991). An exploratory study of secondary LEP programs. *Meeting the challenge of diversity: An evaluation of programs for pupils with limited proficiency in English, Vol. 5.* Berkeley, CA: BW Associates.

Mohan, B. (1986). *Language and content.* Reading, MA: Addison-Wesley.

Moll, L.C. (1988). Some key issues in teaching Latino students. *Language Arts, 65,* 462-472.

Moll, L.C. (1992). Bilingual classroom studies and community analysis: Some recent trends. *Educational Researcher, 21*(2), 20-24.

Moll, L.C., & Greenberg, J.B. (1990). Creating zones of possibilities: Combining social contexts for instruction. In L.C. Moll (Ed.), *Vygotsky and education* (pp. 319-348). Cambridge, England: Cambridge University Press.

Mosher, R.L., & Purpel, D.E. (1972). *Supervision: The reluctant profession.* Boston: Houghton-Mifflin.

National Center for Education Statistics. (1997). *Mini-digest of education statistics, 1996* [NCES 97-379]. Washington, DC: U.S. Government Printing Office.

Nieto, S. (1991). *Affirming diversity: The sociopolitical context of multicultural education.* White Plains, NY: Longman.

Odell, S. (1986). Induction support of new teachers: A functional approach. *Journal of Teacher Education, 37*(1), 26-30.

Oja, S.N. (1991). Adult development: Insights on staff development. In A. Lieberman & L. Miller (Eds.), *Staff development for education in the '90s* (2nd ed.) (pp. 37-60). New York: Teachers College Press.

Pack, A.C. (Ed.). (1970). Video and micro-teaching: Adaptable medium, adaptable method. *TESOL Reporter, 3*(2), 1-2, 11. (ERIC Document Reproduction Service No. ED 184 350)

Pajak, E. (1993). *Approaches to clinical supervision: Alternatives for improving instruction.* Norwood, MA: Christopher-Gordon.

Pease-Alvarez, L., Espinoza, P., & García, E. (1991). Effective schooling in preschool settings: A case study of LEP students in early childhood. *Early Childhood Research Quarterly, 4,* 153-164.

Pink, W., & Hyde, A. (Eds.). (1992). *Effective staff development for change.* Norwood, NJ: Ablex.

Ramirez, J.D., Yuen, S.D., & Ramey, D.R. (1991). *Longitudinal study of structured English immersion strategy, early-exit, and late-exit transitional bilingual education programs for language-minority children.* San Mateo, CA: Aguirre International.

Retallick, J.A. (1990). *Clinical supervision and the structure of communication.* Paper presented at the annual meeting of the American Educational Research Association, Boston.

The road to college: Educational progress by race and ethnicity. (1991). Boulder, CO: Western Interstate Commission for Higher Education and The College Board.

Roberts, S. (1993). *Who we are: A portrait of America based on the latest U.S. Census.* New York: Times Books.

Ross, P. (1994). Preparing teacher educators and prospective teachers to meet the challenge of diversity. In C. Kinzer, D. Leu, J. Peter, L. Ayre, & D. Frommer (Eds.), *Multidimensional aspects of literacy research, theory, and practice. Forty-third Yearbook of the National Reading Conference.* Chicago: National Reading Conference, Inc.

Rugger, K. (1990). A teacher's odyssey. In *Insights: Thought on the process of being International* (pp 36-41). Long Island City: The International High School.

Russell, S.C., Williams, E.W., & Gold, V. (1994, March). Teachers teaching teachers: The art of working together and sharing. In D. Montgomery (Ed.*), Rural partnerships: Working together. Proceedings of the Annual National Conference of the American Council on Rural Special Education (ACRES)*, Austin, TX. (ERIC Document Reproduction Service No. ED 369 616)

Sarason, S.B. (1982). *The culture of the school and the problem of change* (2nd ed.). Boston: Allyn & Bacon.

Schon, D.A. (1983). *The reflective practitioner: How professionals think in action.* New York: Basic Books.

Schon, D.A. (1987). *Educating the reflective practitioner: Toward a new design for teaching and learning in the professions.* San Francisco: Jossey-Bass.

Schwartz, J. (1991). Developing an ethos for professional growth: Politics and programs. In A. Lieberman & L. Miller (Eds.), *Staff development for education in the '90s* (2nd ed.) (pp. 184-192). New York: Teachers College Press.

Senge, P. (1990). *The fifth discipline.* New York: Doubleday.

Short, D.J. (1991). *How to integrate language and content instruction: A training manual* (2nd ed.). Washington, DC: Center for Applied Linguistics.

Shulman, J., & Mesa-Baines, A. (Eds.). (1993). *Diversity in the classroom: A casebook for teachers and teacher education learners.* Philadelphia: Research for Better Schools and Lawrence Erlbaum Associates.

Siens, C.M., & Ebmeier, H. (1996). Developmental supervision and the reflective thinking of teachers. *Journal of Curriculum and Supervision, 11(4)*, 299-319.

Sizer, T. (1984). *Horace's compromise: The dilemma of the American high school.* Boston, MA: Houghton Mifflin.

Smyth, W.J. (1984a). Observation: Toward a 'critical consciousness' in the instructional supervision of experienced teachers. *Curriculum Inquiry, 14*(4), 425-436.

Smyth, W.J. (1984b). Teachers as collaborative learners in clinical supervision: A state-of-the-art review. *Journal of Education for Teaching, 10*(1), 24-38.

Smyth, W.J. (1990, April). *Problematizing teaching through a "critical" approach to clinical supervision.* Paper presented at the annual meeting of the American Educational Research Association, Boston.

Snow, M.A., Met, M., & Genesee, F. (1989). A conceptual framework for the integration of language and content in second/foreign language instruction. *TESOL Quarterly, 23*, 201-217.

Steinberg, S. (1989). *The ethnic myth: Race, ethnicity, and class in America.* Boston, MA: Beacon Press.

Sykes, G. (1990). Fostering teacher professionalism in schools. In R.F. Elmore & Associates, *Restructuring schools: The next generation of educational reform* (pp. 59-96). San Francisco: Jossey-Bass.

Szecsy, E. (1996). *The fractal ecology of diversity: How school leaders make sense of their environment.* Unpublished doctoral dissertation, Teachers College, Columbia University.

Tedick, D.J., & Walker, C.L. (1994). Second language teacher education: The problems that plague us. *The Modern Language Journal, 78*(3), 300-311.

Tedick, D.J., & Walker, C.L. (1995). From theory to practice: How do we prepare teachers for second language classrooms? *Foreign Language Annals, 28,* 499-517.

Tharp, R.G., & Gallimore, R. (1989). *Rousing minds to life: Teaching, learning, and schooling in social context.* New York: Cambridge University Press.

Tikunoff, W.J. (1983). *Compatibility of the SBIF features with other research on instruction of LEP students.* San Francisco: Far West Regional Laboratory.

Torres-Guzmán, M.E., & Goodwin, A.L. (1995). Urban bilingual teachers and mentoring for the future. *Education and Urban Society, 28*(1), 48-66.

Vallance, E. (1983). Hiding the hidden curriculum: An interpretation of the language of justification in nineteenth-century educational reform. In H. Giroux & D. Purpel (Eds.), *The hidden curriculum and moral education: Deception or discovery?* Berkeley, CA: McCutchan. (Original work published 1973/1974)

Van Manen, M. (1977). Linking ways of knowing with ways of being practical. *Curriculum Inquiry, 6,* 205-228.

Villegas, A.M. (1996). Increasing the diversity of the U.S. teaching force. In B. Biddle, T. Good, & I. Goodson (Eds.), *The international handbook of teachers and teaching* (pp. 297-335). The Netherlands: Kluwer Academic.

Wasley, P.A. (1991). The practical work of teacher leaders: Assumptions, attitudes and acrophobia. In A. Lieberman & L. Miller (Eds.),

Staff development for education in the '90s (2nd ed.) (pp. 158-183). New York: Teachers College Press.

Wasser, J.D., & Bresler, L. (1996). Working in the interpretive zone: Conceptualizing collaboration in qualitative research teams. *Educational Researcher, 25*(5), 5-15.

Wilsey, C., & Killion, J. (1982). Making staff development programs work. *Educational Leadership, 40*(1), 36-43.

Wise, A.E., Darling-Hammond, L., & Berry, B. (1987). *Effective teacher selection: From recruitment to retention.* Santa Monica, CA: Rand Corporation.

Wood, F.H., & Thompson, S.R. (1993). Assumptions about staff development based on research and best practice. *Journal of Staff Development, 14*(4), 52-57.

Wright, D.P., McKibbon, M., & Walton, P. (1987). *The effectiveness of the teacher trainee program: An alternate route into teaching in California.* Sacramento: California Commission on Teacher Credentialing.

Zeichner, K.M. (1993). *Educating teachers for cultural diversity. NCRTL special report.* East Lansing, MI: National Center for Research on Teacher Learning. (ERIC Document Reproduction Service No. ED 359 167)

Zeichner, K.M., & Hoeft, K. (1996). Teacher socialization for cultural diversity. In J. Sikula, T. Buttery, & E. Guyton (Eds.), *Handbook of research on teacher education* (2nd ed.). New York: Macmillan.

Zeichner, K.M., & Liston, D.P. (1987). Teaching student teachers to reflect. *Harvard Educational Review, 57*(1), 23-48.

Zelasko, N.F. (1991). *The bilingual double standard: Mainstream Americans' attitudes toward bilingualism.* Unpublished doctoral dissertation, Georgetown University, Washington, DC.

How to order documents from ERIC

Citations with ED numbers are documents from the U.S. Department of Education's *Resources in Education.* They can be read at a library with an ERIC microfiche collection or purchased, in microfiche or paper copy, from: ERIC Document Reproduction Service (EDRS), 7420 Fullerton Rd. Suite 110, Springfield VA 223-2852 (Phone: 800-443-3742) (E-mail: service@edrs.com) (World Wide Web: http://www.edrs.com).

For the location of the nearest ERIC collection, call 1-800-276-9834 or contact the Center for Applied Linguistics, ERIC Clearinghouse on Languages and Linguistics (ERIC/CLL), 1118 22nd St. NW, Washington DC 20037-1214 (Phone: 202-429-9292 ext. 204) (Fax: 202-659-5641) (E-mail: eric@cal.org).

Index

3362